AWS Certified Solutions Architect Associate

The ultimate guide for the SAA-C02 exam

Jonathan Anderson

©Copyright 2020 by Jonathan Anderson

All rights reserved.

This document is geared towards providing exact and reliable information with regards to the topic and issue covered. The publication is sold with the idea that the publisher is not required to render accounting, officially permitted, or otherwise, qualified services. If advice is necessary, legal or professional, a practiced individual in the profession should be ordered.

-From a Declaration of Principles which was accepted and approved equally by a Committee of the American Bar Association and a Committee of Publishers and Associations.

In no way is it legal to reproduce, duplicate, or transmit any part of this document in either electronic means or in printed format. Recording of this publication is strictly prohibited and any storage of this document is not allowed unless with written permission from the publisher. All rights reserved.

The information provided herein is stated to be truthful and consistent, in that any liability, in terms of inattention or otherwise, by any usage or abuse of any policies, processes, or directions contained within is the solitary and utter responsibility of the recipient reader. Under no circumstances will any legal responsibility or blame be held against the publisher for any reparation, damages, or monetary loss due to the information herein, either directly or indirectly.

Respective authors own all copyrights not held by the publisher.

The information herein is offered for informational purposes solely, and is universal as so. The presentation of the information is without contract or any type of guarantee assurance.

The trademarks that are used are without any consent, and the publication of the trademark is without permission or backing by the trademark owner. All trademarks and brands within this book are for clarifying purposes only and are the owned by the owners themselves, not affiliated with this document

Summary

Introduction

For individuals applying for the position of solution architect, the AWS Certified Solutions Architect Associate exam is necessary. This Exam validates a candidate's ability to:

- Identify and collect requirements needed to define a solution which will be modeled according to the best architectural practices.
- Advice developers and system administrators on architectural best practices throughout the project lifecycle.

Your AWS knowledge level can be defined by the following skills or qualities:

AWS knowledge

- Hands-on experience using AWS compute network, storage and database services

- Work experience in designing large-scale distribution systems

- To give insight into the concepts of elasticity and scalability

- Insight into the global AWS infrastructure

- Insight into network technologies related to AWS

- An understanding of all AWS security features and tools and their relationship with traditional services

•   A solid knowledge of customer interfaces with the AWS platform

•   Hands-on experience with AWS implementation and management services.

Studying for a certification exam can seem daunting. This study guide is designed and developed with relevant topics, questions and exercises to enable a cloud practitioner to focus their valuable study time and effort on the relevant set of topics aimed at the appropriate level of abstraction. Thus, they can confidently pass the AWS Certified Solutions Architect - Associate exam.

This book contains questions each to help you gauge your readiness to take the Exam.

Passing the AWS Certified Solutions Architect – Associate exam requires understanding the components and operation of the core AWS services as well as how those services interact with each other. Read through the official documentation for the various AWS services. Amazon offers HTML, PDF, and Kindle documentation for many of them.

Each chapter contains specific information about the service or topic covered, followed by a section on Exam Basics that provides the key information you will need to prepare for your exam. Then, each chapter contains sample questions to familiarize you with answering questions about AWS Cloud services and architecture topics.

If you are looking for a focused book written by solution architects who have written, assessed and developed the AWS Certified Solutions Architect - Associate exam, this book is for you.

Taking the Exam

Once you are fully prepared to take the exam, you can visit the AWS certification site to schedule and pay for your exam:

https://www.aws.training/certification?src=arc-assoc

AWS partners with PSI Exams (https://candidate.psiexams.com), so when you schedule your exam, you'll locate a testing center to take the exam as well as a time block.

The exams typically take two hours, so you'll need to plan accordingly. On the test day, make sure you arrive 10 minutes earlier in case of any hiccups or a long line of folks waiting to take the exam. You'll need two forms of identification too. Remember that your notes, electronic devices (including smartphones and watches) or other materials should not be taken with you.

The testing centre will provide you with scratch papers, and most centres will supply headphones or earplugs if you find it helpful to block out the minimal noises of the testing centre. On a computer, the exam itself is taken and it's reasonably straightforward.

General Computer Knowledge

- Excellent understanding of typical multi-level architectures: web servers, caching, application servers, load balancers and storage
- Equipped with the knowledge of relational database management system (RDBMS) and NoSQL
- Equipped with the knowledge of message queues and Enterprise Service Bus (ESB)
- Equipped with the knowledge of loose links and stateless systems
- Insight into the different consistency models of the distribution systems
- Knowledge of Content Delivery Networks (CDN)
- Hands-on experience with major LAN / WAN network technologies
- Experience with routing tables, access control lists, firewalls, NAT, HTTP, DNS, IP and OSI network
- Equipped with the knowledge of RESTful, XML, JSON web services
- Equipped with the Knowledge of the software development life cycle
- Experience in working with information and application security concepts, mechanisms and tools
- Equipped with the knowledge of end-user computing and collaboration technologies

These training courses or other equivalent methodologies will help with further preparation for the exam:

- Architecture on AWS (aws.amazon.com/training/architect)
- In-depth knowledge of or training in at least one high-level programming language

- AWS Cloud Computing White Papers (aws.amazon.com/whitepapers)
  - Presentation of Amazon Web Services
  - Overview of security processes
  - AWS Risk & Compliance White Paper
  - Cloud storage options
  - Architecture for the AWS cloud: best practices
- Experience in the implementation of on-premise and AWS component hybrid systems
- Using the AWS Architecture Center website (aws.amazon.com/architecture)

Exam objectives

For those with experience in developing software and distribution systems on the AWS platform and plans to take the AWS Accredited Solutions Architect-Associate Exam, here are some of the major exam topics you should be familiar with:

- Design and deploy scalable, available, and fault-tolerant systems on AWS Migrate existing on-premises applications to AWS.
- Data input and output to and from AWS
- Select the correct AWS service based on data, calculations, database or security requirements
- Identifying the Proper Use of AWS Architectural Best Practices
- Estimate the cost of AWS and identify cost control mechanisms

In general, applicants should have:

- One or more years of practical experience in the development of highly open, cost-effective, stable, fault-tolerant, and scalable distributed systems on AWS
- Atleast a thorough knowledge of one high-level programming language.
- Ability to identify and define requirements for an AWS-based application
- Experience in implementing hybrid systems with on-premises and AWS components
- The ability to provide best practices for building secured and reliable applications on the AWS platform

The exam covers four different areas, with each area split into objectives and sub-objectives.

Note: This exam plan includes weightings, test goals, and sample content. Sample topics and concepts are included in order to clarify the objectives of the test; it should not be construed as an exhaustive list of all the contents of the review.

Chapter 1

Introduction to AWS

Amazon Web Services, Inc. (AWS) started delivering IT technology services to organizations in 2006 as web services, more widely referred to as cloud computing. The ability to substitute upfront capital infrastructure costs with low variable costs that scale with your company is one of the main advantages of cloud computing. Companies no longer need to prepare servers and other IT resources and also wait for weeks or months in advance before acquisition. Instead, in minutes, they can spin hundreds or thousands of servers immediately and produce results more efficiently.

AWS today offers a highly secured, scalable, low-cost cloud computing platform that control hundreds of thousands of organizations in 190 countries across the globe.

In this chapter, an introduction to the AWS Cloud computing platform is described. The benefits of cloud computing and the basics of AWS are discussed. It offers a summary of the profoundly essential AWS Cloud resources for the exam.

What is "Cloud Computing"?

Cloud computing has become one of the most talked-about computing paradigms in recent years. It builds on the many advancements in the IT industry over the past decade and offers companies significant opportunities to shorten market time and reduce costs. Cloud computing allows companies to use shared computing and storage resources instead of building, operating and improving their infrastructure themselves. Rapid changes in the markets are putting significant pressure on the company's IT infrastructure to adapt swiftly and be operational. Cloud computing offers new solutions to deal with these changes. As defined by Gartner1, "Cloud computing is a type of computing in which scalable and resilient computing resources are offered to external clients using Internet technology as a service."

Cloud computing enables businesses to create a flexible, secured and cost-effective IT infrastructure, in the same manner that national power grids enable households and organizations connect to a centrally managed, efficient and cost-effective energy source. Once freed from capitalizing on their own abilities, companies can focus on their business core competencies and the needs of their customers. Likewise, cloud computing enables companies to avoid spending valuable time and budget on activities that do not directly contribute to the major aims while still acquiring IT infrastructure capabilities.

These functions include computing power, storage, databases, messaging and other basic services for business applications. Combined with utility-style pricing and business model, cloud computing promises to deliver a reliable, fast, and cost-effective enterprise-class IT infrastructure.

Basically, Cloud computing is an Internet-based computing service that networks large groups of remote servers to allow centralized data storage and access to computing services or resources online.

By using cloud computing, organizations can apply shared computing and storage resources instead of building, operating and improving their own infrastructure.

Cloud computing allows the following functions;.

- Users can provide and release resources on demand.
- Resources are accessible through a network with appropriate security.
- Depending on the load, resources can be automatically increased or decreased.
- A pay-as-you-go model can be launched by cloud service providers, where consumers are billed based on the types and uses of resource.

Amazon and Cloud Computing

Amazon has long applied a decentralized IT infrastructure. This arrangement allowed our development teams to access on-demand computing and storage resources and increase overall productivity and flexibility. By 2005, Amazon had spent more than a decade and millions of dollars building and operating the reliable, large-scale, and efficient IT infrastructure that enabled and supported one of the world's largest online retail platforms.

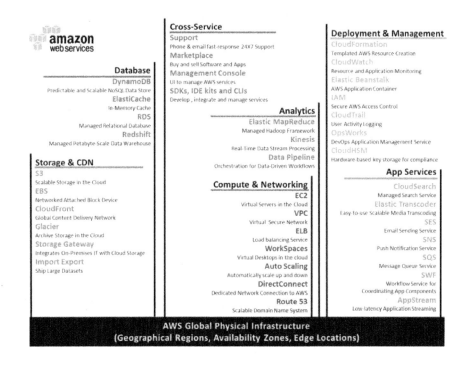

Amazon has launched Amazon Web Services.

(AWS) ensures that other organizations can take advantage of Amazon's experience and investment in managing a large-scale distributed transactional IT infrastructure. AWS has been in use since 2006 and today serve hundreds of thousands of customers around the world. Today, Amazon.com operates a global web platform that serve millions of customers and process billions of dollars in trade every year.

With AWS, you can request computing power, storage, and other services in minutes, and you have the liberty to select the platform or programming creation model that fit the issues to be solved. You can only make payment for what you use, with no upfront costs or long-term commitments, and this makes AWS a cost-effective way to deliver apps.

Here are some examples of how organizations, from research firms to large enterprises, use AWS today:

- A large corporation swiftly and cost-effectively implement new internal applications, such as HR solutions, payroll applications, inventory management solutions, and online training for its distributed workforce.
- An e-commerce website responds to the sudden demand from Facebook and Twitter for a "hot" product launched by the viral buzz, without having to upgrade the infrastructure.
- A research-based pharmaceutical company runs large-scale simulations using computing power from AWS.
- Media companies offer unlimited videos, music and other media to their customers globally.

Types Of Cloud

We have three types of cloud: private, hybrid and public cloud.

1. Private Cloud

A private cloud provides about the same features as the public cloud, but the company or third party controls the data and resources only for the client's company.

2. Hybrid Cloud

The combination of a private and public cloud is called a hybrid cloud.The decision to apply a private or public cloud usually depends on several parameters such as data and application sensitivity, required industry certifications and standards, regulations, etc.

3. Public Cloud

Third-party service providers ensure that tools and services are accessible over the Internet to their users through public cloud. Customer data and associated security are also present within the infrastructure owned by the service providers.

Cloud Service Models

There are three types of Cloud service models: IaaS, PaaS and SaaS.

- IaaS

IaaS stands for Infrastructure as a Service. It allow users provide processing, storage and network connectivity on demand. Using this service model, customers can develop their own applications on these resources.

- PaaS

PaaS stands for Platform as a Service. Here, the service provider offer various services such as databases, queues, workflow engines, email, etc. for their customers. The customer can then use these components to build their own applications. Services, resource availability, and data backup are managed by the service provider, allowing customers focus more on their application's functionality.

- SaaS

SaaS stands for Software as a Service. As the name suggests, the third-party vendors here provide end-user applications for their customers with application-level management capabilities such as creating and managing their users. Some customization level is also possible; for example, customers can use their own logos, colours, etc.

Advantages Of Cloud Computing

Here's a list of some of the main benefits cloud computing has to offer:

- Economical: Building our own servers and tools takes time and is just as expensive as ordering, paying, installing and configuring expensive hardware long before it is needed. However, by using cloud computing, we only pay the main costs and time period for using the computing resources. In this manner, cloud computing remains profitable.
- Reliability: A cloud computing platform offers a better managed, consistent and efficient service than an internal IT infrastructure. Furthermore, 24/7 and 365 days of service are assured. If one of the servers goes down, the hosted applications and services can easily be transferred to any of the available servers.

- Unlimited Storage: Cloud computing offers almost unlimited storage capacity which means that there is no need to worry about running out of storage space or increasing the capacity of the existing storage space. We have access to as little or as much as needed.
- Backup and restore: It is comparatively simpler to save data in the cloud, back it up, and restore than to save it on a physical computer.
- There is also ample technology for cloud service providers to recover our data, so it can be accessible at any time.
- Easy access to information: once you have registered in the cloud, you can access your account from anywhere in the world, as long as internet connection is available. There are several storage and security facilities which vary depending on the type of account chosen.

Disadvantages Of Cloud Computing

While Cloud Computing offers a great array of benefits, it also has drawbacks that often raise questions about its effectiveness.

- **Security concerns.** The biggest issue with cloud computing is stability. Cloud service providers introduce the best security norms and industry certifications, but storing important data and files on third-party service providers can pose certin degree of risks.

The most scalable and stable cloud network built is the AWS cloud infrastructure. It provides a scalable and extremely reliable platform that enable customers to rapidly and securely deploy applications and data.

- **Technical problems.** Because cloud service providers render services to a number of customers on a daily basis, the system can sometimes experience serious problems resulting in a temporary suspension of business processes. Moreover, if there is no access to internet connection, there will be no access to the applications, servers or data in the cloud.

- **Uncertainties in changing service providers.** Cloud service providers promise customers that the cloud will be flexible to use and integrate, however, switiching to cloud services can be difficult. It could be difficult for most organisations to host and implement existing cloud systems on another platform. Certain difficulties can be experienced in interoperability and support, such as applications developed on the Linux platform that may not work properly on Microsoft Development Framework (.Net).

Benefits of AWS security

- Protect your data: The AWS infrastructure does a great job at helping you protect your privacy. In highly secured AWS data centers, all data is effectively stored.
- Meeting compliance requirements: AWS manage dozens of compliance programs in its infrastructure and this imply that parts of your compliance process has been completed.
- Save money: You can reduce costs by using AWS data centers and also maintain the highest level of security without having to manage your own installation.
- Scale quickly: The security system adapts to your AWS Cloud usage. Regardless of the size of your business, the AWS infrastructure is designed to protect your data.

Compliance

AWS Cloud Compliance helps you understand the robust controls used at AWS to maintain data security and ultimately protect your data in the cloud. Since the systems are built on the AWS Cloud infrastructure, compliance responsibilities are shared. By combining governance-focused, audit-friendly service functions with applicable compliance or auditing standards, AWS Compliance Enablers leverage other traditional programs. This help customers set up and operate in an AWS security auditing environment.

The IT infrastructure that AWS offer its clients is built and controlled in compliance with the best security practices and a variety of IT security requirements, Here is a partial list of insurance programs that AWS complies with:

- SOC 1 / ISAE 3402, SOC 2, SOC 3
- FISMA, DIACAP and FedRAMP
- PCI DSS level 1
- ISO 9001, ISO 27001, ISO 27017, ISO 27018

Amazon Web Services Cloud Platform

AWS is a comprehensive cloud service platform that provides the computing power, storage, content delivery, and other functions that businesses can use to deploy applications and services cost-effectively, through flexibility, scalability, and reliability. AWS Self-Service implies that you can proactively process your internal plans and respond to external requests at any point in time.

Computing and Networking

Amazon Elastic Compute Cloud is a web service that provides customizable computing capacity in the cloud. It is designed for developers and system administrators to promote web-scale computing.

Amazon EC2's simple web service interface allows you to acquire and configure capacity with minimal friction. It puts you in full control of your IT resources and lets you run on Amazon's proven IT environment. Amazon EC2 reduces the time it takes to acquire and start a new server, so you can quickly scale the capacity as your IT needs change. Amazon EC2 changes the economics of computers by paying for the capacity you require. Amazon EC2 provide developers and system administrators with the tools needed to build fault-resistant applications and isolate themselves from common fault scenarios.

Automatic Scaling

Auto Scaling allows you to automatically increase or decrease your Amazon EC2 capacity based on your predefined conditions. With Auto Scaling, you can ensure that the number of Amazon EC2 instances you use increase transparently during peak hours to maintain performance and decrease automatically during pauses in demand to minimize costs. Auto Scaling is particularly suitable for applications dealing with variations in hourly, daily or weekly usage.

Autoscaling is powered by Amazon CloudWatch and is available at no additional cost beyond the cost of Amazon CloudWatch.

Elastic Load Balancing

Incoming device traffic is automatically spread through several Amazon EC2 instances through Elastic Load Balancing. By vividly providing the amount of load balancing power required in response to incoming application traffic, you can achieve even greater fault tolerance in your applications. Elastic Load Balancing detects failed instances and redirects traffic to safe instances automatically before fixing the failed instances. Customers can enable Elastic Load Balancing in a single availability zone or enable more consistent application performance in multiple zones.

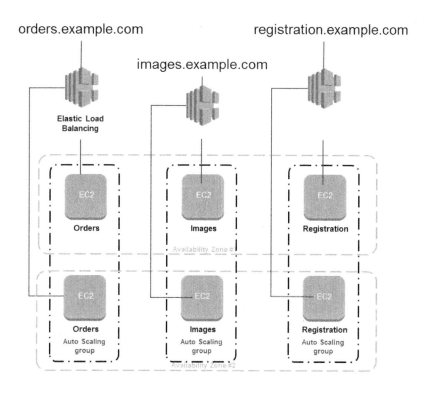

Amazon WorkSpaces

Amazon WorkSpaces is a fully managed, cloud-based IT office service. Amazon WorkSpaces offer cloud-based desktops swiftly to customers, enable end-users to access the documents, apps and tools they need, including laptops, iPads, Kindle Fire or Android tablets, through the computer of their choice. Customers can offer a high quality desktop environment for any number of users at a very reasonable cost relative to conventional desktops and at half the cost of other business solutions with only a few clicks in the AWS Management Console.

Amazon Virtual Private Cloud (Amazon VPC)

Amazon Virtual Private Cloud allows you to possess a logically separated portion of the Amazon Web Services (AWS) cloud where AWS resources can be launched on a given virtual network. You have full control over your virtual network environment, including the selection of your own range of IP addresses, creating subnets, and configuring routing tables and network gateways.

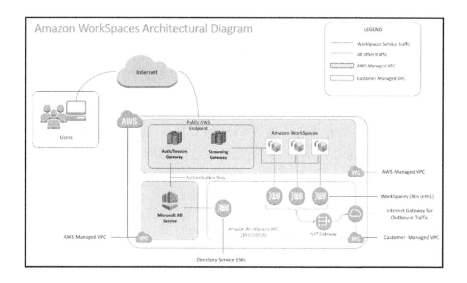

Amazon WorkSpaces Architectural Diagram

You can easily adjust the network configuration of your Amazon VPC. For example, you can create a public subnet for your web servers that have Internet access and place your main systems, such as databases or application servers, in a private subnet without Internet access. You can take advantage of the multiple layers of security (including security groups and network access control lists) to help manage access to the Amazon EC2 instances in each subnet.

In addition, you can establish a hardware connection for a virtual private network (VPN) between your corporate data center and your VPC and take advantage of the AWS Cloud as an extension of your corporate data center.

Amazon Route 53

The Amazon Route 53 is a highly accessible and scalable Domain Name System (DNS) web service. It is designed to provide developers and businesses with an extremely reliable and cost-effective approach for directing end users to Internet applications by translating human-readable names, such as www.example.com, into digital IP addresses, such as 192.0.2.1, which enable computer users to connect with each other. Route 53 links user requests efficiently to the AWS running infrastructures, such as an EC2 case, an elastic load balancer, or an Amazon S3 bucket. It is also possible to use Route 53 to connect users to infrastructure outside the AWS.

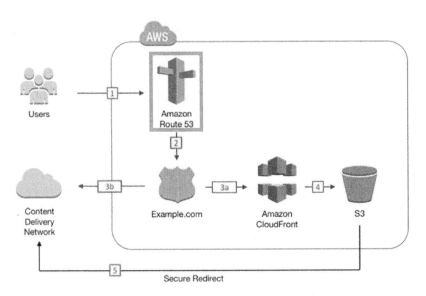

Amazon Route 53 is built to be fast, cost-effective and easy to use. It responds to DNS queries with low latency using a global DNS server network. For the best possible results, queries for your domain are automatically routed to the nearest DNS server. With an easy-to-use API, Route 53 helps you build and manage your public DNS records. It is also compatible with other web services from Amazon. For example, by using the Route 53 AWS Identity and Access Management (IAM) program, you can monitor who make changes to your DNS records in your organization. There are no long-term contracts or minimal usage criteria for using Route 53-like other Amazon web services- you only pay for domain management through the service and the number of requests the service responds to.

AWS Direct Connection

AWS Direct Connect can easily create a dedicated network link between your property and AWS. You can create a private link between AWS and your data center with AWS Direct Connect. This can be achieved in the office or colocation environment and will ultimately minimize the cost of your network and improve bandwidth throughput and offer a more reliable network experience than the Internet.

You can create a dedicated network link between your network and one of the AWS Direct Connect locations using AWS Direct Connect. This dedicated link can be partitioned into several logical links using industry-standard 802.1Q virtual LANs (VLANs). This will give you access to use the same connection in accessing public resources such as public IP address space objects stored in Amazon S3 and private resources such as Amazon EC2 instances in an Amazon VPC using a private IP space while preserving the distinction of networks between public and private environments.

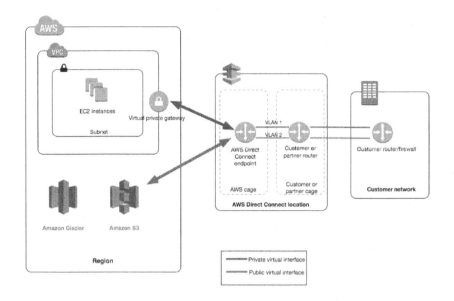

Content Storage And Delivery Network

Amazon Simple Storage Service (Amazon S3)

Amazon S3 is a storage unit for the Internet. It is designed to facilitate web-scale calculations for developers. Amazon S3 offers a simple web services interface that can be used to store and retrieve any amount of data at anytime and anywhere on the Internet. The container is called an Amazon S3 bucket for objects contained in the Amazon S3. Amazon S3 provides every developer with access to similar and highly scalable, reliable, stable, quick, and low-cost infrastructure used by Amazon to run its own global website network. The service aims to maximize economies of scale and pass these benefits on to developers.

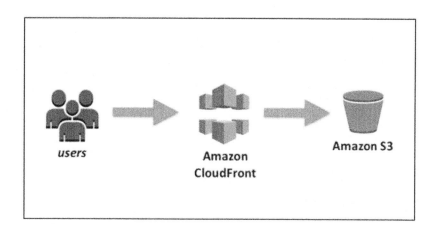

users   Amazon CloudFront   Amazon S3

Amazon Glacier

Amazon Glacier is an extremely cost-effective storage service that provides secured and durable storage for archiving and backing up data. To minimize costs, Amazon Glacier is optimized for data that is not frequently requested and for which recovery time of several hours is required. Amazon Glacier allows customers to reliably store large or small amounts of data for as little as $ 0.01 per gigabyte per month, significantly enhancing savings for local solutions.

Generally, businesses pay huge sum of money to archive data. First, they are forced to make an expensive upfront payment for archiving solution (which does not include the present costs of operating expenses such as electricity, facilities, personnel and maintenance). Second, because businesses have to suggest what their capacity requirements should be, they are naturally over-supplied to ensure that they have adequate data redundancy capacity and appreciable growth.

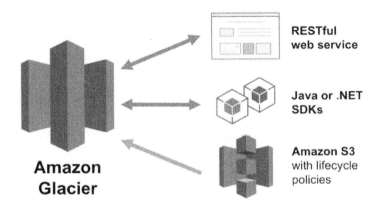

These conditions can lead to underused capacity and wasted capital. With Amazon Glacier, you only pay for what you use. Amazon Glacier is a game-changer when it comes to archiving and backing up data because you don't have to pay anything upfront. You can pay a very low price for storage, and scale your usage as needed, while AWS manages the whole concept. For the operational tasks required for data retention, it takes a few clicks to configure Amazon Glacier in the AWS Management Console; then, you can download any amount of data you require.

Amazon Elastic Block Storage (EBS)

Amazon Elastic Block Store (EBS) provides block-level storage volumes for use with Amazon EC2 instances. Amazon EBS volumes are connected to the network and will persist regardless of the duration of an instance. Amazon EBS offers highly accesible, reliable and predictable storage volumes that can be associated with an active Amazon EC2 instance and displayed as a device within the instance. Amazon EBS is particularly suitable for applications that require a database, file system, or raw block-level storage access.

AWS Storage Gateway

AWS Storage Gateway is a service that links cloud storage to an on-site software appliance to provide seamless and secured connectivity between the on-site IT environment of an enterprise and the storage infrastructure of AWS. For cost-effective backup and speedy disaster recovery, the service enables you to securely upload data to the AWS Cloud. AWS Data Gateway follows industrial-standard data protocols and operates with the current applications. It delivers low-latency performance by retaining data on your on-premises storage hardware while such data is uploaded asynchronously to AWS, Amazon Easy Storage Service (Amazon S3) or Amazon Glacier, where it is encrypted and safely stored.

You can make one-time backup snapshots of your on-premises application data to Amazon S3 for future recovery purposes using the AWS Storage Gateway. If you need disaster recovery replacement capacity, or if you want to use the on-demand computing capabilities of Amazon EC2 for additional capacity during peak periods, you can use the AWS Storage Portal to mirror your on-site data to Amazon EC2 instances for new projects, or as a more cost-effective method of running your regular workloads.

Import/Export AWS

AWS Import / Export accelerates the transfer of vast volumes of data to and from AWS using portable transport storage devices. AWS directly transfers the data over Amazon's internal high-speed network to and from storage devices and also bypasses the Internet. AWS Import / Export is also quicker than internet upload for massive data sets and more cost-effective than updating the connectivity.

Amazon CloudFront

Amazon CloudFront is a web content delivery service. Amazon CloudFront integrates with other Amazon web services to provide developers and businesses with an easy way to distribute content to end-users with low latency, fast data transfer speeds and no strings attached.

Amazon CloudFront can be used to serve your entire website, including dynamic, static and streaming content through a global network of edge locations. Object requests are automatically routed to the nearest edge position to provide the best performing content possible. Amazon CloudFront, such as Amazon S3 and Amazon EC2, is configured to work with other Amazon web services. Amazon CloudFront also operates well for every server of origin, and stores original and final versions of your files. As with other Amazon web services, there is no contract or monthly obligation required to use Amazon CloudFront - you only pay for as much or as little of the content that you provide through the service.

Database

Amazon Relational Database Service (Amazon RDS)

This web service enables you to easily set up, operate, and scale a relational database in the cloud. It provides cost-effective, scalable capacity while handling time-consuming database management tasks, so you can focus on your applications and business.

Amazon RDS provides you with access to trusted MySQL, Oracle, SQL Server or PostgreSQL database functions. This means that Amazon RDS can be used with the code, software and software which is currently inclined with your database today. Amazon RDS automatically restores the database software and backs up your database, storing the backups for the retention period that you set and enabling recovery at a specified period of time. You have the flexibility to scale the compute resources or storage capacity associated with your relational DB instance using a single API call. In addition, Amazon RDS makes it easier to use replication to improve the availability and reliability of production databases and to scale beyond the capacity of a single database implementation for core tasks.

Amazon DynamoDB

Amazon DynamoDB is a swift, fully managed NoSQL database service that makes storing and retrieving any amount of data and serving any level of query traffic simple and cost-effective. All data items are kept on Solid State Drives (SSDs) and replicated for more availability and reliability in 3 availability zones. With DynamoDB, the administrative burden of running and scaling a distributed DB cluster with high availability can be eased while paying a low price for what you need.

Amazon DynamoDB is intended to tackle the key problems of database management, performance, scalability, and reliability.

Developers can generate a database table for storing and retrieving any amount of data and to support any volume of query traffic. DynamoDB automatically distributes data and table traffic across a sufficient number of servers to handle customer-specified demand capacity and the amount of data stored, while maintaining consistent and fast performance. All data items are stored on solid-state drives (SSDs) and are automatically replicated to provide inbuilt high availability and data reliability across multiple availability zones in an area.

Amazon DynamoDB allows customers to lighten the administrative burden of operating and scaling a high-availability distributed DB cluster while paying only a minimal variable price for the resources they need.

Amazon ElastiCache

The Amazon ElastiCache is a web service that allows the easy installation, running and scaling of in-memory cache in the cloud. The service improves web application performance by enabling you to retrieve information from a fast, memory-dependent caching system, rather than relying entirely on slower disk-based databases. ElastiCache supports two open-source caching engines.

- Memcached - A widely adopted caching system for memory objects. ElastiCache is compatible with the Memcached protocol, and therefore, the common tools in use today can seamlessly work with the service in the current Memcached environments.
- Redis- A common in-memory key-value open-source store which supports data structures such as sorted sets and lists. Redis Master/Slave Replication is provided by ElastiCache, which can be used to achieve cross AZ redundancy.

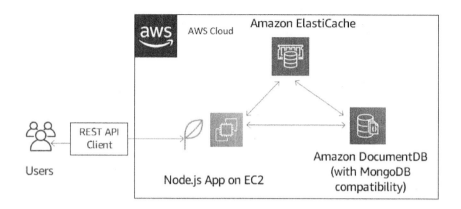

Amazon ElastiCache has the capability to detect and replaces failed nodes automatically, eliminating self-managed infrastructure overhead and offering a robust framework that reduces the risk of overloaded databases which can slow down websites and applications' loading time. By integrating with Amazon CloudWatch, Amazon ElastiCache provides a better understanding of the key performance metrics associated with your Memcached or Redis nodes.

Amazon Redshift

Amazon Redshift is a fast, fully managed, petabyte-scale data warehouse service that enables efficient analysis of all your data in a simple and cost-effective manner using your existing business intelligence tools.

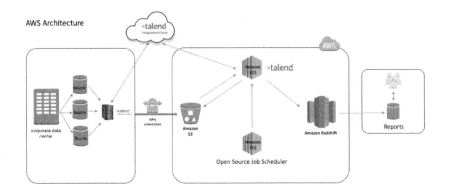

Amazon Redshift delivers fast query and I/O performance for datasets of almost any size by leveraging column storage technology and parallelization and distribution of queries across multiple nodes. By automating many of the common management tasks associated with provisioning, configuring, tracking, backing up, and protecting a data warehouse, we have made Amazon Redshift easier to use.

Furthermore, there are inbuilt strong security features. Amazon Redshift supports VPC out-of-the-box from Amazon, and you can encrypt all your data and backups with just a few clicks. After creating the cluster, you can connect to it and start loading data and running queries with the same SQL tools you are currently using.

Analytics

Amazon Elastic MapReduce (Amazon EMR)

The Amazon Elastic MapReduce (Amazon EMR) is a web service that makes it easy to quickly and cost-effectively process large volumes of data.

To spread information and process through a customizable cluster of Amazon EC2 instances, Amazon EMR uses Hadoop, an open-source infrastructure. Amazon EMR is used in various applications, including log analysis, web indexing, data warehousing, machine learning, financial analytics, science simulation, and bioinformatics. Every year, millions of Amazon EMR clusters are introduced by customers.

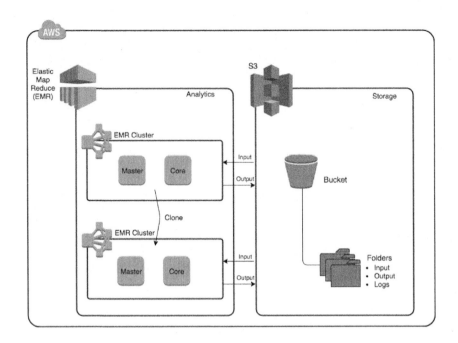

Amazon Kinesis

Amazon Kinesis is a completely operated service for processing large-scale streaming data in real-time. From hundreds and thousands of sources, Amazon Kinesis can capture and process hundreds of terabytes of data per hour., so you can easily write applications that process information in real-time, from sources such as clickstreams. Websites, marketing and financial information, instrumentation manufacturing and social media, operational logs and counting data.

Amazon Kinesis applications allow you to create real-time dashboards, capture exceptions and generate alerts, generate recommendations, and make other business or operational decisions in real-time. Furthermore, you can also easily send data to various other services such as Amazon Simple Storage Service (Amazon S3), Amazon DynamoDB or Amazon Redshift. You can start creating apps with just a few clicks and a few lines of code that react to changes in your data feed in seconds and at any size.

AWS Data Pipeline

The AWS Data Pipeline is a web service that enables you to process and transfer data efficiently at defined intervals between different AWS computing and storage facilities, as well as on-site data sources. You can access your data periodically with the AWS Data Pipeline where it is stored, transformed and processed. AWS providers such as Amazon S3, Amazon RDS, Amazon DynamoDB and Amazon Elastic drive the results quickly and efficiently.

The AWS Data Pipeline makes it easy to build complex, fault-tolerant data processing tasks, which are repeatable and highly available. You don't have to worry about resource availability, managing dependencies between tasks, restarting temporary outages or timeouts during individual tasks, or creating a notification system.

Management Tools

AWS offers a range of resources that help companies control their AWS properties. An overview of the management resources that AWS offer to organizations is provided in this section.

Amazon CloudWatch

Amazon CloudWatch is a tracking tool for AWS Cloud services and AWS-based applications. It enable organizations collect and control metrics, gather and track log files, and set alarms. By leveraging Amazon CloudWatch, organizations can gain system-wide visibility into resource utilization, application performance, and operational health. By using these insights, organizations can react, as necessary, to keep applications running smoothly.

AWS CloudFormation

The AWS CloudFormation offers an efficient method for developers and system administrators to build and manage, provide and upgrade a set of related AWS resources in an orderly and predictable manner. AWS CloudFormation is used to describe a template language based on JSON which influences all AWS resources available for a workload. Templates may be sent to AWS CloudFormation and, in the appropriate order, the service will take care of providing and configuring these tools.

AWS CloudTrail

AWS CloudTrail is a web service that track calls of an account from the AWS API and provides audit and review log files. Documented information includes the API caller's name, the API caller's time, the API caller's source IP address, the parameters of the request, and the response elements returned by the service.

AWS Config Configuration

AWS Config is a completely managed service that provide organizations with an inventory of AWS tools, configuration history, and alerts for configuration changes to enable protection and governance. Organizations can discover existing AWS resources with AWS Config, export an inventory of their AWS resources with all configuration information, and decide at any point in time how a resource has been configured. These capabilities allow auditing of enforcement, security review, tracking of resource changes, and troubleshooting.

Application Services

Amazon AppStream

Amazon AppStream is a low-latency, flexible service that allows you to stream resource-intensive apps and games from the cloud. It deploys and renders your application on the AWS infrastructure and delivers the output to mass-market devices such as personal computers, tablets and cell phones. Because your app runs in the cloud, it can be scaled to meet major computing and storage needs, regardless of the devices your customers use. You can choose to stream all or part of your app from the cloud. Amazon AppStream enables game and application usage scenarios that would not be possible by default on consumer devices. With Amazon AppStream, your games and applications are no longer limited by the hardware in the hands of your customers.

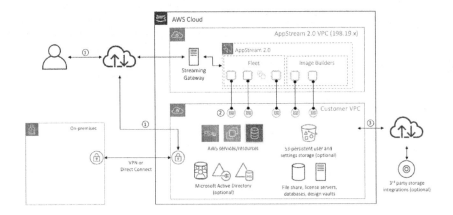

Amazon AppStream includes an SDK that currently supports streaming apps from Microsoft Windows Server 2008 R2 to FireOS, Android, iOS, and Microsoft Windows devices.

Amazon Simple Queue Service (Amazon SQS)

Amazon Simple Queue Service is a swift, reliable, scalable and fully managed message queuing service. SQS simplifies and saves the cost of disconnecting the components of a cloud application. You can use SQS to send any amount of data at any speed level without losing messages or involving other available services.

With SQS, you can lighten the administrative burden of managing and scaling a high-availability message cluster, while paying a low price for mainly what you use.

Amazon Simple Notification Service (Amazon SNS)

Amazon Simple Notification Service (SNS) is a flexible, fast and fully managed push notification service. SNS simplifies and saves transferred data to mobile devices such as iPhone, iPad, Android, Kindle Fire and Internet-connected smart devices and also transfer to other distributed services.

In addition to sending cloud notifications directly to mobile devices, SNS can also send notifications via SMS or email, to Simple Queue Service (SQS) queues or any other HTTP endpoint.

All messages posted on Amazon SNS are stored redundantly in multiple Availability Zones to avoid losing messages.

Amazon Simple Workflow Service (Amazon SWF)

Amazon Simple Workflow Service is a task coordination and health management service provided for cloud applications. With this, you can stop developing complex glue and state machines and invest more in the business logic that makes your applications unique.

Our APIs, easy-to-use libraries and control engine provided developers the tools to coordinate, control, and scale applications across multiple machines - in the AWS Cloud and other data centers. Whether it's automating financial application business processes, building big data systems, or managing cloud infrastructure services, Amazon SWF helps you develop applications with business-resilient processing steps. It can also involve steps that can be scaled and controlled independently of each other, even when they affect different systems.

With Amazon SWF, you can structure the various processing steps in an application that runs on one or more machines as a set of "tasks." Amazon SWF manages the dependencies between tasks, schedules tasks for execution, and executes any logic developed in parallel. The service also store tasks, reliably distributes them across application components, tracks their progress and maintains their latest status.

Amazon SWF makes it easy to adjust application logic as the business requires change, without thinking about the underlying state processes, specialization of duties, and flow control. You only pay for what you use, like other AWS services.

Easy Email Service (Amazon SES) from Amazon

Amazon Simple Email Service is a mass and transactional email service for companies and developers and they are highly scalable and cost-effective. Amazon SES eliminates the difficulty and cost of creating an in-house messaging solution or authorizing, installation and the usage of a third-party messaging service. The service interacts with other AWS systems, making it easy to send emails from services such as Amazon EC2 hosted applications. With Amazon SES, no long-term commitments, minimum expenses or negotiation are required. Organizations can employ a free usage tier and then pay a lower amount for the number of emails sent plus data transfer charges.

Creating large-scale messaging solutions to send marketing and transactional messages is often a complex and costly challenge for businesses. To optimize email delivery's success rate, organizations must handle mail server management and network configuration and adhere to strict Internet Service Providers (ISP) standards for email content. Additionally, many third-party messaging solutions require contract and price negotiations, as well as significant upfront costs.

Amazon SES eliminates these challenges and allows companies to take advantage of the years of experience and advanced messaging infrastructure that Amazon.com has designed to serve its customer base at large. With SMTP or a simple API call, an organization can now access a scalable, high-performance messaging infrastructure to communicate efficiently and cost-effectively with its customers. For high email deliverability, Amazon uses SES content filtering technologies to analyze an organization's outbound email to ensure that it meets ISP standards.

The email is then queued for transmission or returned to the sender for corrections and modifications.. Amazon SES offers a built-in feedback loop, including bounce alerts, unsuccessful and efficient delivery attempts, and spam reports, to help companies further enhance email communication efficiency with their clients.

Amazon CloudSearch

It is a completely managed AWS Cloud service that helps you to quickly set up, manage and scale up a website or application search solution. For large data sets, such as web pages, paper files, forum posts, or product information, Amazon CloudSearch provides opportunities for searching.

You can easily add search features to your website with Amazon CloudSearch without being a research expert or thinking about setting up search functions, configuring and maintaining hardware. You can create a search domain with a few clicks on the AWS Management Console, then upload the data you want to search for to Amazon CloudSearch. The search service automatically provides the required technical resources and implements a highly optimized search index. As your data volume and traffic fluctuate, Amazon CloudSearch seamlessly adapts to your needs. You can easily change your search parameters, refine search relevance and apply new parameters at any time without having to upload your data again.

Amazon CloudSearch relieves customers of the administrative burden and costs of operating and scaling a search service. With Amazon CloudSearch, you don't have to worry about hardware provision, data partitioning or software patches.

Amazon Elastic Transcoder

Amazon Elastic Transcoder is a cloud-based media transcoding. It is designed as a highly scalable, easy-to-use and cost-effective method for developers and businesses to convert (or 'transcode') media files from their source format into versions that can be played on smartphones, tablets and PCs.

Amazon Elastic Transcoder helps you manage all aspects of the transcoding process transparently and automatically. There is no need to manage software, scale hardware, tune performance, or otherwise manage the transcoding infrastructure. You can create a transcoding "job" to specify your source video's location and how you want it transcoded. Amazon Elastic Transcoder also offers to transcode presets for common output formats, meaning you don't have to stress about which settings work best on particular devices. All of these features are available through the service APIs and the AWS Management Console.

Deployment and Management

AWS Identity and Access Management (IAM)

AWS Identity and Access Management (IAM) allows you to securely manage access to your users' AWS services and resources. IAM allows you to create and manage AWS users and groups, and also use permissions to deny their access to AWS resources. With IAM, you can:

- Manage and access IAM users- You can build IAM users, grant individual security credentials to them (i.e., multi-factor access keys, passwords and authentication devices) or request temporary security credentials to allow users access AWS services and resources. You can manage permissions to control what a user can do.
- Manage IAM roles and their permissions: You can create roles in IAM and control permissions to manage the operations performed by the AWS entity or service that

assumes the role. You can also determine which entity can take over the role.

- Manage federated accounts and their permissions- You can enable the identity federation to allow the organization's current identities (e.g., accounts) access the AWS Management Console, call AWS APIs, and also access resources, without requiring an IAM for each identity user.

Amazon CloudWatch

Amazon CloudWatch provides monitoring for AWS cloud resources and the applications which customers run on AWS. In order to keep their applications and companies running smoothly, developers and system managers often use this system to gather and monitor statistics, gain insight and act instantly. Amazon CloudWatch monitors AWS tools such as Amazon EC2 DB Instances and Amazon RDS Instances, and can also monitor custom statistics generated by a customer's applications and services. With Amazon CloudWatch, you gain system-wide insight into resource usage, application performance and operational health.

Amazon CloudWatch offers a reliable, scalable and flexible monitoring solution that can be accessed in minutes. You no longer need to configure, manage or scale your own surveillance systems and infrastructure. By using Amazon CloudWatch, you can easily monitor as much or as little metrics as you need. Amazon CloudWatch allows you to programmatically retrieve your monitoring data, display graphs and set alarms to help you troubleshoot, track trends and take automated action based on the status of your cloud environment.

AWS Elastic Beanstalk

AWS Elastic Beanstalk is an easy-to-use service built-in popular programming languages such as Java, .NET, PHP, Node.js, Python and Ruby for deploying and scaling web applications and services. When you upload the application, Elastic Beanstalk automatically handles capacity provisioning, load balancing, auto-scaling and application status which monitors implementation information. furthermore, you can maintain complete control over the AWS resources that power your application and also, you can access the underlying resources at any time using Elastic Beanstalk.

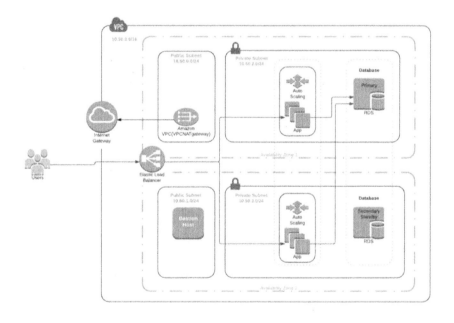

Most existing application containers or platform-as-a-service solutions reduce the amount of programming required, and also significantly reduce developer flexibility and control. Developers are forced to live with all of the vendor's predetermined decisions - with little or no opportunity to regain control of the various parts of their application infrastructure. However, with Elastic Beanstalk, you retain full control over the AWS resources that power your application. If you decide to inherit some (or all) of the infrastructural elements, you can vividly apply the management capabilities of Elastic Beanstalk.

To ensure your application's easy portability, Elastic Beanstalk is designed using well-known application/web servers such as Apache HTTP Server, Apache Tomcat, Nginx, Passenger and IIS 7.5 / 8.

AWS CloudFormation

AWS CloudFormation offers a simple method for developers and system administrators to build and manage various AWS-related tools which were provided and upgraded in an orderly and predictable manner.

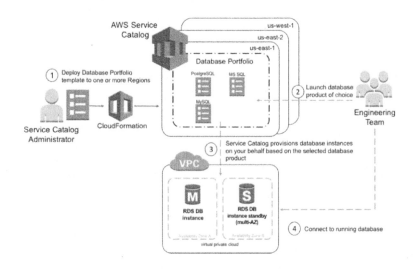

To define the AWS resources and any associated dependencies or runtime parameters needed to run your application, you can use the AWS CloudFormation sample models or build your own. You don't have to determine the order in which AWS services should be delivered or the intricacies of how those dependencies work. AWS CloudFormation will take care of that for you. Once implemented, you can modify and update AWS resources in a controlled and predictable manner. This allows you to manage your AWS infrastructure in the same manner as versioning your software.

You can deploy and update a model and its resource collection (called a stack) using the AWS Management Console, the AWS CloudFormation command-line tools, or the CloudFormation API. AWS CloudFormation is available for free, and you will only pay for the AWS resources required to run your applications.

AWS OpsWorks

AWS OpsWorks is an application management service that enables DevOps users, from load balancers to databases, to easily model and manage the entire application. You can start with templates for popular technologies such as Ruby, Node.JS, PHP and Java, or build your own with Chef Recipes to install software packages and perform whatever tasks that can be written. AWS OpsWorks can scale your application using load-based or time-based autoscaling and maintain your application's integrity by detecting and replacing failed instances. Ultimately, you have full control over the implementations and automation of each part.

AWS CloudHSM

The AWS CloudHSM service helps you meet business, contractual and regulatory compliance requirements for data security by utilizing dedicated Hardware Security Module (HSM) equipment in the AWS Cloud.

AWS and AWS Marketplace partners offer a variety of solutions to protect sensitive data within the AWS platform, but for applications and data with strict contractual or legal requirements for cryptographic key management, additional protection is sometimes required. Until now, the only option you have is to store sensitive data (or the encryption keys that protect sensitive data) in your local data centers. Unfortunately, this will prevent you from moving these apps to the cloud or lead to slowed performance significantly.

With the AWS CloudHSM service, you can protect your encryption keys in HSMs designed and validated by government standards for secured key management. You can securely generate, store, and manage cryptographic keys used for data encryption so that they are only accessible to you. Without compromising application efficiency, AWS CloudHSM lets you meet strict key management requirements.

Amazon Virtual Private Cloud (VPC) operates with the AWS CloudHSM service. CloudHSMs are provided in your VPC with an IP address that you specify, and thus, provides an easy, private network connection to your Amazon Elastic Compute Cloud (EC2) instances. Placing CloudHSMs near your EC2 instances reduces network latency, which can increase the efficiency of the application. AWS offers CloudHSMs unique and dedicated access, which is different from other AWS customers.

Security and Identity

AWS offers protection and identity services that help companies protect their data and systems in the cloud. These high-level resources are discussed in the next segment.

Control of AWS Identity and Access (IAM)

Identity and Access Management (IAM) from AWS helps organizations to securely control their users ' access to AWS Cloud services and resources. Organizations can build and manage AWS users and groups using IAM and also use permissions to allow or deny AWS resource accesibility.

Main Management Service for AWS (KMS)

The AWS Key Management Service is a managed service that makes it easy for organizations to build and maintain encryption keys used to encrypt their data and they secure these keys using hardware protection modules (HSMs). To help secure data stored with these services, AWS KMS is integrated with many other AWS Cloud services.

AWS Directory Service

With AWS Directory Service, organizations can configure and run Microsoft Active Directory on the AWS Cloud or connect their

AWS resources to an existing on-premises Microsoft Active Directory. Organizations can use it to handle users and groups, provide apps and facilities with a single sign-on, build and enforce community policies, join the domain of Amazon EC2 instances, and deploy and manage Linux simplify workloads and cloud-based Microsoft Windows

AWS Certificate Manager

AWS Certificate Manager is a service that enables the use of Stable Sockets Layer / Transport Layer Protection (SSL/TLS) certificates with AWS Cloud services which can be easily delivered, controlled and deployed by the organizations.

It eliminates the tedious manual process of SSL/TLS certificates being purchased, downloaded and renewed. Organizations can easily request a certificate using AWS Certificate Manager, deploy it to AWS tools such as Elastic Load Balancing or Amazon CloudFront distributions, and allow AWS Certificate Manager handle certificate renewals.

AWS Web Application Firewall (WAF)

WAF (AWS Web Application Firewall) helps secure web applications from major attacks and vulnerabilities that can affect the availability of applications, compromise security or consume unnecessary resources.With AWS WAF, organizations can control the type of traffic allowed on the web applications or blocked by defining customizable web security rules.

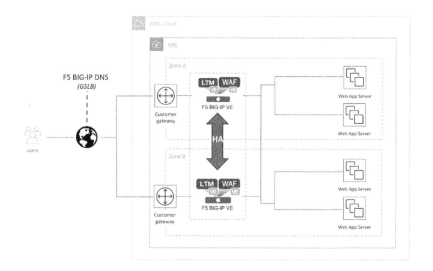

"Cloud computing" refers to the on-demand accessibility of computing services for a charge peruse over the Internet. Companies can purchase technology such as computing power, storage, databases and other resources as required, instead of purchasing, owning and running data centers and servers.

With several locations around the world, AWS provides a highly accessible technological infrastructure network. These locations consists of the regions and areas of availability. This allows organizations to place resources and data in multiple locations around the world. Thus, it helps to protect the confidentiality, integrity, and availability of systems and as data is paramount to AWS, it helps maintain the trust of several organizations around the world.

AWS offers a wide variety of global compute, storage, database, analysis, application and implementation services that help

53

organizations scale faster, reduce IT costs and scale applications. Having a broad understanding of these services enables solution architects to design efficient distributed systems and applications on the AWS platform.

Exam Essentials

➢ Understand the global infrastructure. With several locations around the world, AWS provides a highly accessible technological infrastructure network. These locations are made up of regions and various availability areas. Each region is situated in a different geographical area and has many isolated locations called zones of availability.

➢ Understand the regions. A geographical area is made up of a cluster of data centers is an AWS area. AWS regions allow resources and data to be positioned in multiple locations around the world. Each region is fully autonomous and totally separated from other regions. This guarantees the greatest tolerance and reliability of faults which might be encountered. Unless organizations want to do so, services are not replicated across these regions.

➢ Understand the Areas of Availability. A zone of availability is one or more data centers in an area intended to be separated from outages in other zones of availability. Availability zones provide low-cost, low-latency network connectivity for other zones in the same region. By placing assets in separate availability zones, businesses can protect their website or application from service disruption in one location.

➢ Understand the hybrid deployment model. A hybrid deployment model is an architectural model that provides connectivity for infrastructure and applications between cloud resources and existing resources that are not present in the cloud.

Assessment Test

Question 1

Within 30 days, a business must move 20 TB of data from a data center to the AWS Cloud. The corporate network's bandwidth is limited to 15 Mbps and may not exceed 70% of the usage. What must a solution architect do to meet these requirements?

Options:

A. Use AWS DataSync.

B. Use AWS Snowball.

C. Use a secure VPN connection.

D. Use Amazon S3 transfer acceleration.

Answer: B

Question 2

A company's website runs behind an application load balancer (ALB) on Amazon EC2 instances. Users around the world complain that the website is sluggish and has a combination of dynamic and static content.

Options:

A. Build an ALB Amazon Route 53 latency-based log, then start new EC2 instances with larger sizes and log the instances with the ALB.

B. In the regions nearest to the customers, host the website in an Amazon S3 bucket and delete the ALB and EC2 instances. Then, update a record of Amazon Route 53 to point to the S3 buckets.

C. Begin with Nev. EC2 instances in various regions which are near the users host on the same web application. Then, register the instances using multi-region VPC peering with the same ALB.

D. Build a distribution for Amazon CloudFront, configure ALB as the source, and then update the Amazon Route 53 record to point to the CloudFront distribution.

Answer: D

Question 3

A business has an application with a REST-based interface that can collect data from an external provider in real-time. Once received, the app processes the data and stores it for further analysis. The application runs on Amazon EC2 instances. The third-party vendor received numerous 503 service errors that were unavailable while sending data to the app. As the volume of data increases, the computing capacity reaches its maximum limit, and the application cannot process all requests. What design should a solution architect recommend to provide a more scalable solution?

Options:

A. Use Amazon Kinesis data streams to include processed data using AWS Lambda functions.

B. Use Amazon API Gateway in addition to the existing application. Create a usage plan with a quota limit for the third-party provider.

C. To include data, use the Amazon Simple Notification Service (Amazon SNS) and position EC2 instances behind an Application Load Balancer in an Auto Scaling community.

D. Repack the application as a container. Deploy the app with Amazon Elastic Container Service (Amazon ECS) using the EC2 start type with an Auto Scaling group.

Answer: A

Question 4

A business that hosts its web application on AWS requires all Amazon EC2 instances to be protected. Tags are used to configure Amazon RDS DB instances and Amazon Redshift clusters. The organization needs to hold to a minimum, the effort to configure and manage this power. What must a solution architect do to achieve this?

Options:

A. Use AWS configuration rules to define and discover unclaimed resources.

B. Write API calls to verify that all resources are properly allocated. Run the code on an instance of EC2 periodically.

C. Use Cost Explorer to view resources that are not correctly labeled. Mark these sources manually.

D. Write API calls to verify that all resources are properly allocated. Schedule an AWS Lambda feature through Amazon CloudWatch to run code periodically.

Answer: B.

Question 5

A company is running an online transaction processing (OLTP) workload on AWS. This workload employs an unencrypted Amazon RDS DB instance in a Multi-AZ implementation. Daily snapshots of the database are taken from this copy. What should a solution architect do to ensure that the database and snapshots are always encrypted in the future?

Options:

A. Encrypt a copy of the last database snapshot. Replace the existing DB instance by restoring the encrypted snapshot.

B. Create a new Amazon Elastic Block Store (Amazon EBS) encrypted volume and copy the snapshots to it. Enable encryption on the DB instance.

C. Copy the snapshots and enable encryption using AWS Key Management Service (AWS KMS). Restore an encrypted snapshot to an existing DB instance.

D. Copy the snapshots to an Amazon S3 bucket encrypted with server-side encryption using AWS Key Management Service (AWS KMS) and Managed Keys (SSE-KMS).

Answer: A

Question 6

A solution architect must design a well-managed storage solution for an enterprise application that includes high-performance machine learning. This app runs on AWS Fargate, and connected storage must have simultaneous file access and high performance. What storage option should the Solutions Architect recommend?

Options:

A. Create an Amazon S3 bucket for the app and set up an IAM role for Fargate to communicate with Amazon S3.

B. Create an Amazon FSx for Luster file share and set up an IAM role that allows Fargate to communicate with FSx for Luster.

C. Create an Amazon Elastic File System (Amazon EFS) file share and set up an IAM role that allows Fargate to communicate with Amazon EFS.

D. Create an Amazon Elastic Block Store (Amazon EBS) volume for the application and set up an IAM role that allows Fargate to communicate with Amazon EBS.

Answer: B.

Question 7

A company does not have a file sharing service. A new project requires access to file storage that can be mounted as a local workstation disk. The file server must authenticate users on an Active Directory domain before they can access storage. What service can Active Directory users mount the storage as a disk on their desktop?

Options:

A. Amazon S3 Glacier

B. AWS DataSync

C. AWS Snowball Rim

D. AWS storage gateway

Answer: D

Question 8

A company has implemented a website on AWS. The database backend is hosted on Amazon RDS for MySQL with one primary instance, and five read replicas to support scaling requirements. Read replicas should not be delayed for more than 1 second from the primary instance to support the user experience; as website traffic continues to increase, replicas lag further behind for peak periods, leading to user complaints when searches return inconsistent results. A solution architect must keep replication time to a minimum, with minimal changes to application code or operational requirements. Which solution meets these requirements?

Options:

A. Migrate the database to Amazon Aurora MySQL, Replace MySQL, Read Replicas with Aurora Replicas and enable Aurora Auto Scaling.

B. Deploy an Amazon ElastiCache for Redis cluster in front of the database. Edit the website to check the cache before requesting the database read endpoints.

C. Migrate the database from Amazon RDS to MySQL running on Amazon EC2 compute instances. Choose larger machine-optimized instances for all replica nodes.

D. Migration of the database to Amazon DynamoDB will initially provide a large number of reading capacity units (RCUs) to support the required throughput with capacity scaling enabled

Answer: B.

Question 9

A company stores call data on a monthly basis. Statistically, the recorded data can be accessed randomly within the year but it is rarely viewed after one year. Files older than a year should be requested and retrieved as soon as possible. A delay in getting older files is acceptable. A solution architect must store recorded data at a minimal cost. Which solution is the most cost-effective?

Options:

A. Store individual files in Amazon S3 Glacier and store search metadata in object tags created in S3 Glacier Query S3 Glacier tags and retrieve files from S3 Glacier.

B. Keep individual files in Amazon S3 and use lifecycle policy to move files to Amazon S3 Glacier after one year. Search and retrieve files from Amazon S3 or S3 Glacier.

C. Archive individual files and store search metadata for each archive in Amazon S3. Use lifecycle policy to move files to Amazon S3 Glacier after one year.

D. Check-in individual files in Amazon S3 and use lifecycle policy to move files to Amazon S3 Glacier after 1 year. Store metadata in

Amazon DynamoDB, retrieve files from DynamoDB and Amazon S3 or S3 Glacier.

Answer: B.

Question 10

A company's website provides users with downloadable historical performance reports. The website needs a solution that is scalable to meet the requirements of the company's website worldwide. The solution must be profitable and it must be provided at fastest possible response time. What combination should a solution architect recommend to meet these requirements?

Options:

A. Amazon CloudFront and Amazon S3

B. AWS Lambda and Amazon Dynamo

C. Application Load Balancer with Amazon EC2 Auto Scaling

D. Amazon Route 53 with internal application load balances

Answer: A

Related Study Guide: What is a Learning Path?

In different cloud computing fields, the Cloud Academy provides a broad range of video classes, quizzes, and hands-on labs. Our learning routes will help you get to your destination from your present position. The Sol Arch Associate Education Path is your major AWS Certified Solutions Architect - Associate study guide.

In order to help you pass the AWS certification test, our Architect-Associate Learning Path solution include all classes, labs and quizzes you need.

- Every material on the learning path has a different learning goal:
- Video courses provide guided lectures, with examples, on the main sections of the exam.
- Hands-on Labs provide AWS facilities with direct access to help you put the theory into practice.
- A preliminary review gives you the opportunity to assess your abilities and practice before taking the final exam.

The Architect of Solutions-Associate Learning Journey focuses on 4 related fields., each with a percentage weight in the exam:

- Designing resilient architectures (30%)
- Designing high-quality architectures (28%)
- Designing secure applications and architectures (24%)
- Designing cost-optimized architectures (18%)
- Using the learning path
- Understanding your knowledge gaps is an essential part of the AWS Certified Solutions Architect - Associate study guide.

The Solution Architect - Associate learning journey naturally builds on the fundamentals of AWS into more advanced areas. For the best approach, start with the first lesson and continue step by step. Complete each activity to ensure you are familiar with basic computing, storage, database, networking, and security services. As you progress through the learning path, you will be exposed to hands-on labs where you can apply the lessons learnt.

How long will it take?

This is a natural question. To pass the exam, you need to be well prepared, and the duration will depend on your own experience and knowledge.

On average, we recommend approximately 35-40 hours of preparation for the Solutions Architect - Associate exam, provided you have some AWS experience. This includes going through all of your resources, including our Solutions Architect training and any other resource of your choice. The expenditure of 40 hours of study will take 6 to 8 weeks with a full-time job and other commitments.

We suggest that you practice about 50 to 60 hours or for three months if you are completely new to AWS so that you can showcase your knowledge in some of the courses and labs more than once in your weakest areas.

Chapter 2

Easy Storage Service from Amazon (Amazon S3) and Storage for Amazon Glacier

This chapter will help you understand Amazon Simple Storage Service (Amazon S3) and Amazon Glacier, the main object storage services available on AWS.

Amazon S3 offers stable, reliable and extremely scalable cloud storage for developers and IT teams. With a simple web service interface, Amazon S3 is a simple-to-use object storage that can be used to store and retrieve any amount of data, anywhere on the Internet. Amazon S3 also enables you pay only for the storage you use, eliminating the capacity planning and capacity constraints associated with traditional storage.

Amazon S3 was among the first services introduced by AWS. It serves as one of the most important web services: almost all applications run on AWS using Amazon S3, whether directly or indirectly. Amazon S3 can be used alone or in combination with other AWS services, as with many other AWS cloud services as it provides a very wide range of integration. For instance, for Amazon Kinesis and Amazon Elastic MapReduce (Amazon EMR) snapshots, Amazon S3 serves as the durable target storage and it is used as the snapshot storage for Amazon Elastic Block Store (Amazon EBS) and Amazon Relational Database Service (Amazon RDS). Furthemore, it is used as a data storage platform or loading mechanism for Amazon Redshift and Amazon DynamoDB, among many other functions. Due to the flexibility of Amazon S3 and its high integration level and usability, it's important to understand the service in detail.

Common usage scenarios for Amazon S3 storage are:

- Data backup and archiving on-premises or in the cloud
- Storage and distribution of content, media and software
- Big data analysis
- Static website hosting
- Hosting of native mobile and internet applications in the cloud
- Disaster recovery

To support these and more usage options, Amazon S3 offers a range of storage classes designed for a variety of common use scenerios: general use, infrequent access, and archiving. To help manage data throughout its lifecycle, Amazon S3 offers configurable lifecycle policies. By using these lifecycle policies, you can automatically migrate your data to the most suitable storage class, without changing your application code. To control who can access your data, Amazon S3 offers a comprehensive set of permissions, access controls, and encryption options.

Amazon Glacier is another cloud storage service linked to Amazon S3 but optimized for data archiving and long-term backup at an extremely low cost. Amazon Glacier is suitable for "cold data," that is, data that is not requested often and for which a recovery time of three to five hours is acceptable. Amazon Glacier can be used both as an Amazon S3 storage class (see Storage Classes and Object Lifecycle Management in the Amazon S3 Advanced Features section) and as an independent archiving storage service (see Amazon Glacier section).

Traditional Block and File Storage versus Object Storage

In traditional computing environments, two types of storage dominate: bulk storage and file storage. Block storage operates at a lower level - the raw storage device level - and manages data as a set of numbered blocks of fixed size. File storage functions at a higher level (level of the operating system) and handles data as a named file and folder hierarchy. Block and file storage is often network-accessible in the form of a Storage Area Network (SAN) for block storage, using protocols such as iSCSI or Fiber Channel, or as a Network Attached Storage (NAS) file server or "filer" for file storage, using protocols such as Common Internet File System (CIFS) or Network File System (NFS). Whether directly attached or connected to the network, bulk or file, this type of storage is closely related to the server and operating system that uses the storage.

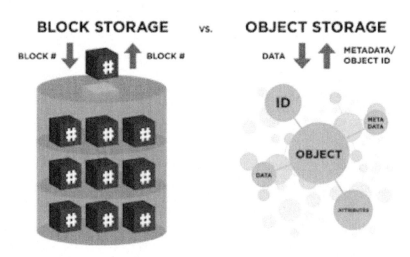

Saving Amazon S3 objects is quite another form. Amazon S3 is used for object storage in the cloud. Rather than being closely tied to a

68

server, Amazon S3 storage is server-independent and accessible from the Internet. Rather than managing data as blocks or files with SCSI, CIFS or NFS protocols, data is managed as objects using an application program interface (API) based on standard HTTP verbs.

Both data and metadata can be found in any Amazon S3 object. Objects reside in containers called buckets, and a specific user-specified key (filename) identifies each object. Buckets are plain flat folder with no hierarchy in the file system. You can possess several buckets but you cant own a sub bucket. An infinite number of things can carry any bucket.

An Amazon S3 object is easy to illustrate, like a file and the Key as a file name. Bear in mind, however, that Amazon S3 is not a conventional file system and varies substantially. You GET an object or Place an object on Amazon S3, then, you can work on the entire object at once instead of incrementally updating parts of the object like you would with a file. You cannot "mount" a bucket, "open" an object, install an operating system on Amazon S3, or run a database on it.

Rather than a file system, Amazon S3 is very durable and highly scalable object storage optimized for reading and designed with an intentionally minimalist feature set. It provides a simple and robust file storage abstraction that frees you from many of the underlying details that you would normally encounter in traditional storage.

You don't have to worry about durability or data replication between availability zones - Amazon S3 objects are automatically replicated to multiple devices across multiple installations in the same region. The same goes for scalability: if your request speed is steadily increasing, Amazon S3 automatically distributes buckets to support very fast request speeds and also allows simultaneous access by many customers.

AWS provide options for a conventional block or file storage in addition to Amazon S3 storage. The Amazon EBS service provides block-level storage for instances of Amazon Elastic Compute Cloud (Amazon EC2). Amazon Elastic File System (AWS EFS) provides network shared file storage (NAS storage) using the NFS v4 protocol.

Amazon Simple Storage Service (Amazon S3) Basics

Now that you have the basic understanding of some of the major differences between two simple storage in the cloud, let's explore the basics of Amazon S3 in more detail.

Buckets

A bucket is a container (web folder) stored on Amazon S3 for objects (files). A bucket normally consists of an Amazon S3 object. For Amazon S3, buckets are the top-level namespace, and bucket names are always global. This implies that, much like the Domain Name System (DNS) domain names, and not just within your account, your bucket names must be identical to all AWS accounts. Up to 63 numbers, lowercase letters, hyphens and periods can be used to create bucket names. You can create and use multiple compartments and you can also have up to 100 per standard account.

It is highly recommended to use bucket names containing your domain name and which also comply with the DNS name rules. This ensures that your bucket names are yours, can be used in all regions, and can also host static websites.

AWS Regions

Although the Amazon S3 bucket namespace is global, each Amazon S3 bucket is created in a specific region of your choice. This allows you to monitor where you store your data. To reduce latency, you can build and use buckets that are near a specific collection of end-users or customers, or in a particular region to address data location and sovereignty issues, or away from your core facilities to enable disaster compliance recovery and compliance needs. You can also determine the location of your data; data from an Amazon S3 bucket can be stored in that region unless you explicitly copy it to another bucket in a different region.

Objects

In Amazon S3 containers, objects are the entities or files stored. In any format, an object can store nearly any type of data. Item sizes can vary from 0 to 5 TB bytes, and an infinite number of objects can be found in a single bucket. This implies that Amazon S3 can save an almost infinite amount of data.

Furthermore, an object is made up of data (the file itself) and metadata (the file data). An Amazon S3 object's data section is invisible to the Amazon S3. This means that the data of an object can be treated as a single stream of bytes. Amazon S3 doesn't know or care about what type of data you are storing, and the service doesn't work differently for text data and binary data.

A list of name/value pairs that can be used to identify the object is similar to the metadata associated with an Amazon S3 object. There are two kinds of metadata: metadata from the device and metadata from the user. Amazon S3 itself generates and uses device metadata and includes items such as last updated date, object size, MD5 digest, and a form of HTTP content. User metadata is optional and can be defined when an object is being created. You can tag the data with attributes that are relevant to you using custom metadata.

Keys

A unique identifier called a key identifies each object stored in a S3 bucket. The Key can be thought of as a file name. A key can contain up to 1024 bytes of Unicode UTF-8 characters, including built-in slashes, backslashes, periods, and hyphens.

Keys must be unique within the same compartment, but different compartments can contain similar Key. The bucket, Key, and optional version ID combination can be used to uniquely identify an Amazon S3 object.

Object URL

Amazon S3 is a storage for web, and each Amazon S3 object can be addressed by a unique URL that is the web services endpoint, bucket name, Key and object. For instance, with the URL:

- HTTP:/mybucket.s3.amazonaws.com / jack.doc Mybucket is the S3 bucket's name, and the main or file name is jack.doc. If a different object is made, such as:
- HTTP:/mybucket.s3.amazonaws.com / fee / fi / fog / smoke / jack.doc.com then, the bucket name is still mybucket but now the key or filename is string.
- fresh / fi / fo / fum / jack.doc. A key can contain delimiting characters such as forward slashes or backslashes that can help you name and logically organize your Amazon S3 objects, but for Amazon S3, it involves just a long key name in a flat namespace. There is no real hierarchy of files and folders. For more information, see the "Prefixes and Separators" topic in the "Amazon S3 Advanced Features" section that follows.

For added convenience, the Amazon S3 console and the Prefix and Separator feature lets you navigate an Amazon S3 bucket as if they were arranged in folders' hierarchy. Note, however, that a bucket with unorganized keys is a single, flat namespace.

Operations of Amazon S3

The Amazon S3 API, with only a handful of common edits, is easy to use. They include:

- Creating/deleting a bucket

- Write an Entity
- Reading an object
- Delete an item
- List of keys inside a compartment

REST Interface

A REST API (Representational State Transfer) is the native interface for Amazon S3. With the REST interface, you can use regular HTTP or HTTPS requests to build and delete buckets, list keys, and read and write objects. By default, REST maps HTTP "verbs" (HTTP methods) to typical CRUD operations (Create, Read, Update, Delete). Create is HTTP PUT (and sometimes POST); reading is HTTP GET; delete is HTTP DELETE, and the update is HTTP POST.

For quality assurance to ensure that your requests and data are safe, always use HTTPS for Amazon S3 API requests.

Users do not explicitly apply the REST interface in most situations but communicate with Amazon S3 through one of the available top-level interfaces. These include the AWS SDKs (wrapper libraries) for iOS, Android, JavaScript, Java, .NET, Node.js, PHP, Python, Ruby, Go and C ++, the interface command line (CLI), and the AWS Management Console.

Amazon S3 originally supported a Simple Object Access Protocol (SOAP) API in addition to the REST API, but you must apply the

REST API. The old HTTPS endpoint is still available, but new features are not supported.

Durability and Availability

Durability and data availability are related, but are slightly different concepts. Sustainability answers the question, "Will my data still be available in the future?" Availability answers the question, "Can I access my data now?" Amazon S3 is designed to deliver your data with high degree of reliability and availability.

In a given year, Amazon S3 Standard Storage is built for 99.99999999999 per cent longevity and 99.99 per cent item availability. For example, if you store 10,000 Amazon S3 objects, on average, you can expect the loss of one object every 10,000,000 years. By automatically storing data redundantly across multiple devices in multiple installations and in the same area, Amazon S3 can achieve high durability. It is designed to withstand simultaneous data loss in two installations without losing user data. Amazon S3 offers a highly durable storage infrastructure designed for the storage of critical and primary data.

Suppose you want to store non-critical or easily reproducible derived data (such as thumbnail of images) that do not require this high level of durability, you can use Reduced Redundancy Storage (RRS) for a low fee. RRS offers 99.99% durability with a lower storage cost than traditional Amazon S3 storage.

Although Amazon S3 storage offers very high durability at the infrastructural level, it is still recommended to provide protection against accidental deletion or overwriting of data at the user level by taking advantage of additional monitoring features which include Version control, cross-regional replication and removal of MFA.

Data Consistency

Amazon S3 is ultimately a cohesive system. As your data is automatically replicated to multiple servers and locations in a region, it can take a longer period of time for your data changes to propagate to all other locations. Therefore, in this situation, the information you read immediately after an update can result in outdated data.

This is no problem in using PUTs for new objects: in this case, Amazon S3 offers read-after-write consistency. However, to use PUTs for existing objects (overwrite object to an existing key) and for DELETE objects, Amazon S3 provides final consistency.

Any consistency means that if you put new data on an existing key, a subsequent GET can return the old data. Likewise, if you DELETE an object, another GET for that object can still read the deleted object. Either way, single key updates are atomic - for consistent reads to the end, you can obtain new data or old data, but never an inconsistent mix of data.

Access Control

Amazon S3 is secured by default; when you create a bucket or an object in Amazon S3, only you can have access to it. To enable you grant others controlled access, Amazon S3 provides both coarse-grained access controls (Amazon S3 access control lists [ACL]) and fine-grained access-controls (Amazon S3 Bucket Policies, AWS Identity and Access Management (IAM) Policies and Query String Authentication).

Amazon S3 ACLs allow you to grant such coarse-grained permissions at an object or bucket level: READ, WRITE, or FULL CONTROL. ACLs are an old system of access control produced before IAM existed. Today, ACLs are best used for a limited number of usage cases, such as enabling bucket logging or creating a bucket that hosts a static, globally readable website.

In place of a primary IAM, they are connected to the bucket resource. They include in the policy, an explicit reference to the primary IAM. This principle can be associated with another AWS account so that you can assign multi-account access to Amazon S3 resources using Amazon S3 Bucket Policy.

With an Amazon S3 bucket policy, you can decide who can access the bucket, from where (by classless cross-domain routing block [CIDR] or IP address) and at a particular time of day.

Finally, IAM policies can be directly associated with primary IAMs that grant access to an Amazon S3 bucket, just as they can offer any

AWS service and resource access. Clearly, you can only delegate IAM policies to AWS account customers that you control.

Static Website Hosting

A common usage case for Amazon S3 storage involves hosting static websites. Many websites, especially microsites, do not require the services of a full web server. A static website means that all pages on the website contain only static content and do not require any processing on the server such as PHP, ASP.NET or JSP. (Note that this doesn't mean that the website cannot be interactive and dynamic; it can be achieved with client-side scripting such as JavaScript embedded in static HTML web pages.) There are several benefits to static websites: they are very fast, highly scalable and are more secure than a traditional dynamic website. Hosting a static website on Amazon S3 can also take advantage of the security, durability, availability and scalability of Amazon S3.

Since every Amazon S3 object has a URL, converting a bucket into a website is relatively easy. To host a static website, you need to configure a bucket for website hosting and then upload the static website content to the bucket.

To configure an Amazon S3 bucket to host static websites:

- Create a bucket with the same name as the hostname of the desired website.
- Download the static files to the bucket.

- Make all files public (readable worldwide).
- Enable static website hosting for the bucket. This includes specifying an index document and an error document.
- The website is now available at the S3 website URL: <bucket-name> .s3-website- <AWS-region> .amazonaws.com.
- Create a friendly DNS name in your own domain for the website using CNAME DNS or an Amazon Route 53 alias that matches the Amazon S3 website URL.
- The website is now available under the domain name of your website.

Amazon S3 Advanced Functions

Also, for the basics, there are some advanced features of Amazon S3 that you should also familiarize yourself with..

Prefixes and Separators

Although Amazon S3 uses a flat structure in a bucket, it supports the use of prefix and separator parameters when listing key names. This functionality allows you to organize, browse, and retrieve the objects in a bucket in a hierarchical manner. Typically, you should use a forward slash (/) or a backslash (\) as a separator and then, use key names with embedded separators to emulate a hierarchy of files and folders in the key namespace. a flat object of a compartment.

For example, you want to store a series of server logs by server name (such as server42), but organized by year and month, as follows:

Logs / January 2016 / Server42.logs

Logs / February / 2016 / server42.log

Logs / 2016 / March / 42.log server

The REST API, the Encapsulation SDKs, the AWS CLI, and the Amazon Management Console all support the use of separators and prefixes. This feature allows you to organize new data logically and easily manage the hierarchical folder and file structure of existing data downloaded or backed up from traditional file systems. When used with IAM or Amazon S3 bucket policies, prefixes and delimiters can also help create the equivalent of department "subfolders" or "home directories" of users in a single bucket, restricting or sharing access to those "subfolders" (defined by prefixes) as required.

Use object separators and prefixes to organize objects in your Amazon S3 buckets hierarchically, but keep in mind that Amazon S3 is really not a filesystem.

Storage Classes

Amazon S3 provides a number of storage classes that are sufficient for various usage cases.

Amazon S3 Standard provides high reliability, high availability, low latency and high-quality object storage for general use. As it offers low latency in the first byte and high throughput, the Standard is preferable for short or long term storage of frequently used data. For most general usage cases, it is best to start with Amazon S3 Standard.

The Amazon S3 Standard-Infrequent Access (Standard-IA) provides the same longevity, low latency, and high performance as the Amazon S3 Standard, but it is designed for long-life data and less-accessed data. Standard-IA has a lower storage cost per GB monthly than the Standard, but the pricing model also includes a minimum object size (128 KB), the minimum duration (30 days), and recovery cost per GB, so it is best suited to rarely access data stored for more than 30 days.

Reduced Redundancy Storage (RRS) from Amazon S3 provides slightly lower reliability (4 new) at a reduced cost than Normal or Normal-IA. It is most suitable for derived data, such as image thumbnails, that can be easily replicated.

Finally, for data that does not require real-time access, such as archives and long-term backups, the Amazon Glacier storage class provides reliable, robust and highly cost-effective cloud storage. To keep costs down, Amazon Glacier is optimized for minimally-used data with a recovery time of several hours. To restore an Amazon Glacier object, issue a restore command with one of the Amazon S3 APIs; three to five hours later, the Amazon Glacier object is then copied to Amazon S3 RRS. Note that the restore option will simply make a copy on the Amazon S3 RRS; the original data object remains in Amazon Glacier until it is explicitly deleted. Also, it is important to note that Amazon Glacier allows you to retrieve up to 5% of the Amazon S3 data stored in Amazon Glacier for free every month. For restorations outside the daily meal allowance, costs for delivery has been made available.

Amazon Glacier is not only used as a storage tier in Amazon S3, but it is also a stand-alone storage service with a separate API and unique functions. However, when you use Amazon Glacier as the Amazon S3 storage class, you can still communicate with data through Amazon S3 APIs. See the Amazon Glacier section for details.

Set a data recovery policy to limit recovery for the free tier or to a maximum limit of GB per hour to avoid or minimize Amazon Glacier recovery costs.

Object Lifecycle Management

Managing the lifecycle of Amazon S3 objects is roughly equivalent to exhausting automated storage in the traditional IT storage infrastructures. In many cases, data has a natural life cycle, starting with "hot" (frequently accessed) data, moving to "hot" (less frequently accessed) data as it ages, and ending with "hot" data. It then moves to Cold" data (backup or long-term archive) before possible deletion.

For example, many business documents are often viewed as they are created, and are hardly viewed over time. In many cases, however, compliance rules require that business records be archived and kept accessible for years. Likewise, studies show that file, operating system, and database backups are most often opened within the first few days of being created, usually to remove an accidental error. After a week or two, these backups will remain a critical asset, but they are much less likely to be accessible for recovery. Compliance laws require a variety of copies to be held for many years in many cases.

With the use of Amazon S3 lifecycle configuration rules, you can reduce your storage costs by automatically transferring data from one storage class to another or even automatically removing the data after a period of time. For example, the backup data lifecycle rules can be:

- Initially saving the backup data in Amazon S3 Standard.
- Switching to Amazon Standard-IA after 30 days.
- After 90 days, begin transition to Amazon Glacier.
- Remove after 3 years.

Lifecycle configurations are linked to the bucket and can apply to all objects in the bucket or only objects specified with a prefix.

Encryption

Encrypting all confidential data contained in Amazon S3, both in flight and at rest, is highly suggested.

Amazon S3 Stable Sockets Layer (SSL) API endpoints can be used to encrypt the Amazon S3 data on the fly. This implies that when in transit over HTTPS, all data sent to and from Amazon S3 is encrypted.

You can use multiple server-side encryption (SSE) variants to encrypt your Amazon S3 data at rest. Amazon S3 encrypts the data at the object level as it writes it to its data centers' drives, and decrypts it for you as you access it. All SSEs run by Amazon S3 and AWS Key Management Service (Amazon KMS) use the advanced 256-bit encryption standard (AES). You can also use client-side encryption to encrypt your Amazon S3 data when at rest, where your data is encrypted for the client before it is sent to Amazon S3.

SSE-S3 (AWS managed keys)

It is a fully integrated "checkbox" encryption solution in which AWS manages key management and key protection for Amazon S3. With a unique key, each object is encrypted. A separate master key then encrypts the real object key itself. At least once a month, a new master key is released, with AWS running the keys. On secure hosts, encrypted data, encryption keys, and master keys are all stored separately, further improving security.

SSE-KMS (AWS KMS keys)

It is a fully integrated solution where Amazon manages and protects your keys for Amazon S3, but you can manage the keys. SSE-KMS offers several additional advantages over SSE-S3. There are different permissions required to access the master key by using SSE-KMS, and this helps to prevent unauthorized access to your Amazon S3 stored items and also adds an additional layer of control. AWS KMS also offers auditing, so you are familiar with whoever is using the key to access objects and time of object access. AWS KMS also allows you to view all unsuccessful attempts to access data by users who were not allowed to decrypt the information.

SSE-C (keys provided by the customer)

This is used if you want to keep your own encryption keys, but don't want to manage or deploy your own client-side encryption library. With SSE-C, AWS performs encryption/decryption of your objects while retaining full control over the keys used to encrypt/decrypt the objects in Amazon S3.

Client-Side Encryption

Client-side encryption refers to the process of encrypting the data on the client-side of your application before it is sent to Amazon S3. To use data encryption keys, you can follow these options:

- Use a customer master key managed by AWS KMS.
- Use a master key on the client-side.

When you use client-side encryption, you retain full control of the encryption process, including the management of encryption keys.

You can also use server-side encryption with keys operated by AWS (SSE-S3 or SSE-KMS) for optimum flexibility and ease of use.

Versioning

By maintaining different versions of an object in the bucket, marked by a unique version ID, Amazon S3 Versioning helps protect the data from unintentional or intentional deletion. Versioning allows any version of an object stored in your Amazon S3 bucket to be preserved, retrieved, and restored. If a user makes a change unintentionally or even deletes an object in your S3 bucket maliciously, you can restore the object back to its source by simply referring to the version ID next to the bucket and the key.

Versioning at the level of the bucket is allowed. Until this is allowed, it is not possible to delete the version from the bucket as it cannot be suspended.

MFA Delete

MFA Delete adds an extra layer of data protection in addition to bucket version management. MFA Delete requires additional authentication to permanently delete an object version or change the version control status of a bucket. MFA Delete requires an authentication code created by a hardware or virtual appliance multi-factor authentication (MFA), in addition to your usual security credentials. Please note that the root account can only enable MFA deletion.

Pre-signed URLs

All Amazon S3 objects are private by default. This means that only the owner has access. However, by creating a pre-signed URL, the object owner may optionally share objects with other individuals, using their own security credentials to grant time-limited permission to download the objects. When creating a predefined URL for your object, you must provide your security credentials and provide a bucket name, object key, HTTP method (GET to download the object). Pre-signed URLs are only valid for the specified length of time. This is especially useful in forming protection against "content scraping" of web content, such as media files stored in Amazon S3.

Multipart Upload

To further support the downloading or copying of large objects, Amazon S3 provides the multipart download API. This allows you to download large objects in parts, as it generally provides better network usage (via parallel transfers), the ability to pause and resume, and the ability to download objects with unknown sizes. .

Multipart download is a three-step process: start, share, download, and finish (or abort). The parts can be downloaded independently in any order, possibly with retransmission. After all, parts are uploaded, Amazon S3 assembles the parts to create an object.

In general, you should use a multipart download for objects larger than 100MB, and objects larger than 5GB. If you are using low-level APIs, you need to download the file in parts and keep track of the parts. When using the high-level APIs and high-level Amazon S3 commands in the AWS CLI (AWS s3 cp, AWS s3 mv and AWS s3 sync), the multipart Upload is automatically required for large objects.

You can set up an object lifecycle policy for a bucket to prevent incomplete multiple downloads after a specified number of days. This minimizes the storage costs associated with multipart downloads that have not been completed.

Range GET

It is possible to download only part of an object (GET) in Amazon S3 and Amazon Glacier using the Range GET. By using the HTTP range header in the GET request or equivalent parameters in one of the SDK wrapper libraries, you can specify the byte range for the object. This can be useful in dealing with large objects if you have a bad connection, or for downloading only a known portion of a large Amazon Glacier backup.

Interregional Replication

Interregional Replication is a feature on Amazon S3 that allows you to asynchronously replicate all new objects from the source bucket in one AWS region to a target bucket in another region. All metadata and ACLs associated with the object are also part of the replication. After configuring cross-regional replication on your source bucket, any change to an object's data, metadata, or ACL will trigger a new replication to the target bucket. To enable cross-regional replication, versioning must be enabled for the source and target buckets, and you must use an IAM policy to allow Amazon S3 replicate objects on your behalf.

Cross-regional replication is often used to reduce the latency required to access objects in Amazon S3 by moving the objects closer to a group of users or to meet the requirements for storing backup data outside the source data. If enabled in an existing bucket, replication between regions will only replicate new objects. Existing objects are not replicated and must be copied to the new compartment via a separate command.

Logging

You can enable Amazon S3 server access logs to monitor requests for your Amazon S3 bucket.

By default, Logout is disabled but can be easily allowed. When you allow bucket logging (the source bucket), you need to choose where the logs (the target bucket) should be stored. The access logs may be placed in the same bucket or in another bucket. In any case, it is optional (but for good practice) to provide a prefix such as logs / or yourbucketname / logs / which will make it easier to identify your logs.

When enabled, logs are delivered with a slight delay at best. The logs contain information such as:

- Applicant account and IP address
- Bucket name
- Ask for time
- Response status or error code
- Action (GET, PUT, LIST, etc.)

Event Notifications

In response to actions taken on items uploaded or stored on Amazon S3, Amazon S3 event notifications may be sent. In response to changes made to the objects stored on Amazon S3, event notifications allow you to run workflows, submit warnings, or take other actions. You can use Amazon S3 event alerts to configure triggers to perform actions when they are downloaded, such as transcoding media files, processing data files when available, and synchronizing objects related to Amazon S3 with other data stores.

Amazon S3 event notifications are configured at the bucket level, and it can be configured through the Amazon S3 console, through the REST API, or using an AWS SDK. Amazon S3 can post notifications when new objects are created (by a PUT, POST, COPY, or multipart upload completion), when objects are deleted (by a DELETE), or when Amazon S3 detects that an RRS object was lost. You can also configure event notifications based on prefixes and suffixes of object names. Notification messages can be sent via Amazon Simple Notification Service (Amazon SNS) or Amazon

Simple Queue Service (Amazon SQS) or directly to AWS Lambda to invoke AWS Lambda functions.

Best Practices, Models And Performance

It is common to use Amazon S3 storage in hybrid computing environments and applications. For example, data from local file systems, databases and compliance archives can be easily backed up over the Internet to Amazon Glacier or Amazon S3, while the main application or database storage remains on-premise.

Another common model involves using Amazon S3 as a bulk "blob" storage for data, while an index of that data is maintained in another service, such as Amazon DynamoDB or Amazon RDS. This allows for quick and complex searches for key names without constantly listing the keys.

Amazon S3 automatically scales to support very fast request rates, automatically repartitioning your buckets as needed. See the Amazon S3 best practice guidelines in the Developer Guide if you need request rates in excess of 100 requests per second. In addition, it is better to maintain a degree of random key distribution, for example, by using a hash as a prefix for key names, to support higher request rates.

Suppose you're running Amazon S3 in a GET-intensive mode, such as static website hosting, for the best performance. In this case, you should consider using an Amazon CloudFront distribution as the caching tier for your Amazon S3 bucket.

Archives

Data is kept in the archives of the Amazon Glacier. An archive can contain up to 40 TB of data, and you can possess an infinite number of archives. Upon creation, every archive is assigned a unique archive ID (You can't define a descriptive archive name, unlike an Amazon S3 object key).

Vaults

Containers for libraries are known as chests. There can be up to 1000 vaults in each AWS account. By using IAM policies or vault access policies, you can monitor access to your vaults and the actions that are permitted.

Vault Locks

You can easily implement and enforce compliance checks for individual Amazon Glacier vaults with a vault lockout policy. You can make specification controls such as Write Once Read Many (WORM) in a vault lockout policy and lock such policy against future changes. Once locked, the policy cannot be changed.

Data Recovery

You can get up to 5% of your data stored in Amazon Glacier daily for free every month. If you recover more than 5%, you will have to pay a recovery fee based on your maximum recovery rate. To eliminate or minimize these costs, you can set a data recovery policy for a vault to limit your recovery actions to free tier or to a certain data rate.

Amazon Glacier and Amazon Simple Storage Service (Amazon S3)

Amazon Glacier is similar to Amazon S3 but differs in several important aspects. Amazon Glacier supports archives of 40 TB versus objects of 5 TB in Amazon S3. Amazon Glacier archives are identified by system-generated archive IDs, Although Amazon S3 allows you use key names that are "secure". The Amazon Glacier archives are automatically encrypted, while the rest of the encryption is optional for Amazon S3. However, by using Amazon Glacier as an Amazon S3 storage class with object lifecycle policy, you can use the Amazon S3 interface to take full advantage of Amazon Glacier's benefits without learning a new interface.

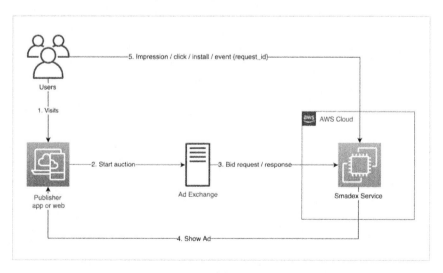

Amazon S3 is the primary object storage service on AWS and it allows you to store an unlimited amount of data with very high durability.

Common usage cases for Amazon S3 include backup and archiving, web content, big data analytics, static website hosting, hosting of mobile and cloud-native applications, and disaster recovery.

Other AWS cloud services, including AWS IAM, Amazon EBS, AWS KMS, Amazon EC2, Amazon EMR, Amazon DynamoDB, Amazon Redshift, Amazon SQS, AWS Lambda, and Amazon CloudFront, are integrated into Amazon S3.

Object storage differs from the traditional block and file storage. Block storage manages device-level data as addressable blocks, while file storage manages OS-level data in the form of files and folders.

Object storage handles data as objects that are accessible by an API, containing both data and metadata.

The Amazon S3 buckets are containers used for storing items in the Amazon S3. Globally, bucket names are often unique. Each bucket is generated in a specific region and, unless the user directly copies it, the data does not leave the region.

Pre-signed URLs enable time-limited permission to download objects and can be used against illegal "site scraping" to protect media and/or other web content.

Multipart Upload is used to upload large items, and portions of an Amazon S3 or Amazon Glacier archive can be uploaded with Range GETs.

Server access logs can be bucket enabled to track requester, subject, action, and response.

When an object is generated or removed, Amazon S3 event notifications may be used to send an Amazon SQS or Amazon SNS message or trigger an AWS Lambda function.

In Amazon S3, Amazon Glacier can be used as a standalone service or a storage class.

Exam Essentials

- Understand what Amazon s3 is and what it is commonly used for. Amazon S3 is a secure, durable and highly scalable cloud storage that can be used to store unlimited amounts of data in almost any format using a simple web services interface. Common usage cases include backup and archiving, content storage and distribution, big data analytics, static hosting of websites, cloud hosting of native software, and disaster recovery.

- Understand how storing objects varies from storing blocks and data. Object storage in the Amazon S3 cloud manages application-level data as objects using a HTTP-based REST API. Block Storage manages OS-level data in numbered addressable blocks using protocols such as SCSI or Fiber Channel. Disk storage handles data using protocols such as CIFS or NFS as OS-level shared files.
- Understand the Amazon S3 basics. Amazon S3 stores data in data and metadata-containing objects. A user-defined key identifies objects and is stored in a simple flat folder called a compartment. Native REST interfaces, multi-language SDKs, and AWS CLI and an AWS Management Console are included in the interfaces.
- Know how to create a bucket; how to upload, download, and remove objects; how to make public objects; and how to open the URL of an object.
- Understand the Amazon S3 model of data durability, availability and consistency. Amazon S3 Standard Storage is designed to last 11 nine and four nine objects in one year. The other storage classes differ. In the end, Amazon S3 is stable but provides new artifacts with read-after-write compatibility for PUTs.
- Know how to enable Amazon S3 for hosting static websites. On Amazon S3, you need to create a bucket with the website hostname to construct a static website, upload your static content and make it public, allow static website hosting on the bucket, and define index and error page objects.
- On Amazon S3, learn how to protect your data. Encrypt data with HTTPS on-the-fly and with SSE or client-side

encryption at rest. Enable versions to hold different versions of an object in the bucket.

- In order to protect against accidental deletion, allow MFA Delete, using the ACL bucket policy for Amazon S3 and the access control policy for AWS IAM. For temporary download access, use pre-signed URLs. To copy data automatically to another region, use replication between regions.

- Be familiar with the usage case for each of the storage classes for Amazon S3. Data requiring high reliability, high performance, and low latency access are commonly used for general purposes. Standard-IA is available for uncommonly used data, but when accessed, it demands the same performance and availability. For easily replicable data, RRS offers lower durability at a lower cost. When the recovery time of three to five hours is appropriate, Amazon Glacier makes it possible to store infrequently used archive data at a lower cost.

- Know how to use configuration laws for the lifecycle. You can configure lifecycle rules in the AWS Management Console or in the APIs. Lifecycle configuration rules define actions for transfering objects from one storage class to another over time.

- Know how to use event alerts from Amazon S3. Event notifications are sent at the bucket level and can trigger an Amazon SNS or Amazon SQS message or an AWS Lambda action in response to an object's upload or delete.

- As a standalone operation, you know the basics of the Amazon Glacier. Data is stored in encrypted archives that can be as wide as 40 TB. Usually, archives contain TAR or ZIP files. Vaults are archive containers, and for compliance, vaults may be closed.

Review Questions

1. You need a low-latency platform where you can store files to be mounted within multiple VPC-based instances. Which of the following AWS services is the best choice?

A. AWS Storage Gateway

B. AWS S3

C. Amazon Elastic File System

D. AWS Elastic Block Store

2. What is the maximum size of S3 object metadata?

A. 2 KB

B. 5 GB

C. 100 MB

D. 5 TB

3. When planning your data operations, it's important to understand the practical limitations you'll encounter. Which of the following will be available only in limited amounts?

A. PUT requests/month against an S3 bucket

B. The volume of data available per S3 bucket

C. Account-wide S3 storage space

D. The number of S3 buckets within a single account

4. You have a publicly available file called filename, stored in an S3 bucket named bucket name. Which of the following addresses will successfully retrieve the file using a web browser?

A. https://s3.amazonaws.com/bucketname/filename

B. https://filename/bucketname.s3.amazonaws.com

C. s3://bucketname/filename

D. s3://filename/bucketname

5. If you want the files stored in an S3 bucket to be accessible using a familiar directory hierarchy system, you'll need to specify prefixes and delimiters. What are prefixes and delimiters?

A. A prefix is the name common to the objects you want to group, and a delimiter is the bar character (|).

B. A prefix is the DNS name that precedes the amazonaws.com domain, and a delimiter is the name you want to give your file directory.

C. A prefix is the name common to the objects you want to group, and a delimiter is a forward slash character (/).

D. A prefix is the name common to the file type you want to identify, and a delimiter is a forward slash character (/).

6. You want to encrypt the objects at rest in an S3 bucket using keys provided by AWS that also allows you to track related events. Which combination of tools would you use?

A. Server-side encryption with AWS KMS-Managed Keys

B. Service-side encryption with Amazon S3-Managed Keys

C. Client-side encryption with AWS KMS-Managed Keys

D. Client-side encryption with Amazon S3-Managed Keys

7. Which of the following operational details are likely to be included in S3-generated logs? (Choose three.)

A. Source bucket name

B. Action requested

C. Current bucket size

D. Response status

8. The S3 data durability guarantees cover which of the following possible threats?

(Choose two.)

A. User misconfiguration

B. Account security breach

C. Infrastructural failure

D. Data center security breach

9. Which of these explains the difference in durability between S3's S3 One Zone-IA and Reduced Redundancy classes?

A. One Zone-IA is heavily replicated but only within a single availability zone, while reduced redundancy is only lightly replicated.

B. Reduced redundancy is heavily replicated but only within a single availability zone, while One Zone-IA is only lightly replicated.

C. One Zone-IA is replicated across AWS regions, while reduced redundancy data is restricted to a single region.

D. One Zone-IA data is automatically backed up to Amazon Glacier while reduced redundancy remains within S3.

10. Which of the following is the 12-month availability guarantee for the S3 Standard-IA class?

A. 99.99 per cent

B. 99.9 per cent

C. 99.999999999 per cent

D. 99.5 percent

11. For which of the following data operations would you not worry about eventual consistency?

A. Operations immediately preceding the deletion of an existing object

B. Operations subsequent to updating of an existing object

C. Operations subsequent to the deletion of an existing object

D. Operations subsequent to the creation of a new object

12. What must you do to protect objects in S3 buckets from being accidentally overwritten?

A. Nothing. S3 protects existing files by default.

B. Nothing. S3 saves older versions of your files by default.

C. Enable versioning.

D. Enable file overwrite protection.

13. How can you apply transitions between storage classes for certain objects within an S3 bucket?

A. By specifying particular prefixes when you define your lifecycle rules

B. This isn't possible. Lifecycle rules must apply to all the objects in a bucket.

C. By specifying particular prefixes when you create the bucket

D. By importing a predefined lifecycle rule template

14. Which of the following classes will make the most sense for long-term storage when included within a sequence of lifecycle rules?

A. Glacier

B. Reduced Redundancy

C. S3 One Zone-IA

D. S3 Standard-IA

15. Which of the following are the recommended methods for providing secured and controlled access to your buckets? (Choose two.)

A. S3 access control lists (ACLs)

B. S3 bucket policies

C. IAM policies

D. Security groups

Answer to Review Questions

1. C. S3 can be used to share files, but it doesn't offer low-latency access—and its eventual consistency will not work well with file systems. Storage Gateway is designed to simplify backing up archives to the AWS cloud; it's not meant for sharing files. EBS volumes can only be used for a single instance at a time.

2. A. Object metadata contains information used by S3 to manage an object's security profile, behaviour, and the manner in which it is exposed to client requests. Storing this information requires very little space—2 KB is normally more than enough.

3. D. In theory, at least, there's no limit to the data you can upload to a single bucket or to all the buckets in your account or to the number of times you upload (using the PUT command). By default, however, you are allowed only 100 S3 buckets per account.

4. A. HTTP (web) requests must address the s3.amazon.aws.com domain along with the bucket and filenames.

5. C. A The prefix is a name common to objects that you want to group, and it is possible to use a slash character (/) as a delimiter. The bar character) (will be viewed not as a delimiter, but as part of the name.While DNS names can have prefixes, they're not relevant to S3 naming.

6. A. Client-side encryption addresses encryption before an object reaches the bucket (i.e., before it rests). Only AWS KMS-Managed Keys provide an audit trail.

7. A, B, D. Since there is no limit to the size of an S3 bucket, there would be little to gain by reporting its current size.

8. C, D. The S3 guarantee only covers the physical infrastructure owned by AWS.

9. A. One Zone-IA can be heavily replicated but only within a single availability zone, while reduced redundancy is only lightly replicated.

10. B. The S3 Standard-IA (Infrequent Access) class is guaranteed to be available 99.9 per cent of the time.

11. D. S3 can't guarantee instant consistency across their infrastructure for changes made to existing objects, but there aren't such concerns for newly created objects.

12. C. Object versioning must be manually enabled for each bucket before older versions of objects will be saved.

13. A. S3 lifecycle rules can incorporate specifying objects by the prefix. There's no such thing as a lifecycle template.

14. A. Glacier offers the least expensive and most resilient storage within the AWS ecosystem. Reduced Redundancy is not resilient, and same apply to S3 One Zone and S3 Standard.

15. B, C. ACLs is a legacy feature that isn't as flexible as IAM or S3 bucket policies. Security groups are not used equally with S3 buckets.

Chapter 3

Amazon Virtual Private Cloud

Amazon Virtual Private Cloud (Amazon VPC) allows you to launch AWS resources in a personally defined virtual network. This virtual network is very similar to the conventional network of your own data centre that you can run, by using AWS's scalable infrastructure.

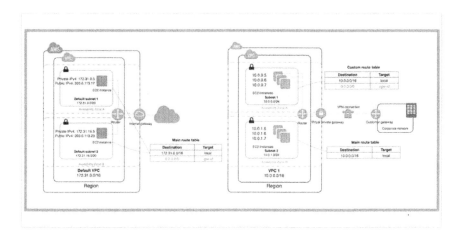

Amazon VPC Concepts

Amazon VPC is the network layer of Amazon EC2. If you are new to Amazon EC2, check out the concept of Amazon EC2, For a quick description, see the Amazon EC2 User Guide for Linux Instances.

These are the main concepts of VPCs:

- Virtual Private Cloud (VPC)- a vitual network for your AWS account only.
- Subnet-The IP address set of your VPC.

107

- Routing table: A set of rules called routes that are used to determine where network traffic is routed.
- Internet Gateway - A gateway that you associate with your VPC to enable communication between your VPC resources and the Internet.
- VPC Endpoint - Enables you to privately connect your VPC to supported AWS services and PrivateLink powered VPC endpoint services without needing an internet gateway, NAT computer, AWS Direct Link connection or VPN connection. To interact with certain services, the instances in your VPC do not require public IP addresses. Traffic does not exit the Amazon network between your VPC and the other provider.

Access to Amazon VPC

You can create, access and manage your VPCs using any of the following interfaces:

- AWS Management Console - Provides a web interface that you can use to access your VPCs.
- AWS Command Line Interface (AWS CLI)-Offers commands and it is supported on Windows, Mac and Linux for a wide range of AWS services, including Amazon VPC. See AWS Command Line Interface for more detail.
- AWS SDKs - Provides language-specific APIs and supports many connection details, such as calculating signatures, handling request attempts, and handling errors. See AWS SDK for more information.
- Request API - Provides behaviour assessment at the lower level of the API which you invoke with HTTPS requests. The most direct way to navigate Amazon VPC is to use the Question API, however, it requires your application to handle low-level details such as generating the hash to sign the

request and handle errors. See the Amazon EC2 API reference for more information.

Amazon VPC Prices

No added costs are associated with using Amazon VPC. You pay standard rates for the instances and other Amazon EC2 features you use. Certain costs are associated with using a site-to-site VPN connection, PrivateLink, traffic mirroring, and a NAT gateway.

Amazon VPC Quota

There are quotas for the number of Amazon VPC components you can provide. You can request an increase for some of these quotas.

PCI DSS Compliance

Amazon VPC supports the processing, storage and transmission of credit card information by a merchant or service provider, and has been validated as compliant with the Industry Data Security Standard (DSS) and Payment cards (PCI).

Amazon VPC offers several network connectivity options that you can use based on your current network designs and requirements. These connectivity options involve using the Internet or an AWS Direct Connect connection as the backbone of the network and terminating the connection to AWS or user-managed network endpoints. In addition, AWS allows you to choose how network routing is provided between Amazon VPC and your networks, taking advantage of AWS or user-managed network equipment and routes.

User network connectivity options for Amazon VPC

- AWS Managed VPN - Describes how to establish a VPN connection between your network equipment on a remote network and the AWS managed network equipment connected to your Amazon VPC.
- AWS Direct Connect - Describes how to establish a private logical connection between your remote network and Amazon VPC using AWS Direct Connect.
- AWS Direct Connect + VPN - Describes how to establish an encrypted private connection between your remote network and Amazon VPC, using AWS Direct Connect.
- AWS VPN CloudHub - Describes how to set up a star model for connecting remote branches.
- Software VPN - Describes how to establish a VPN connection between your equipment on a remote network and a user-managed software VPN device running on an Amazon VPC.
- Transit VPC - Describes the set up of a global transit network on AWS using a software VPN in conjunction with a VPN managed by AWS.

Amazon VPC–to–Amazon VPC Connectivity Options

- VPC Peering – Describes the AWS recommended approach for connecting multiple Amazon VPCs within and across regions using the Amazon VPC peering feature.
- Software VPN - Describes the connection between multiple Amazon VPCs using VPN connections between user-managed VPN software devices running within each Amazon VPC.
- Software Managed VPN with AWS - Describes the connection between multiple Amazon VPCs with a VPN connection established between a user-managed software VPN device in an Amazon VPC and AWS managed network equipment connected to the other Amazon VPC.
- AWS Managed VPN - Describes the link between multiple Amazon VPCs, using multiple VPN connections between your remote network and each of your Amazon VPCs.
- AWS Direct Connect - Describes the connection between multiple AmazonVPCs, using logical connections on customer-managed AWS Direct Connect routers.
- AWS Private Link - Describes the connection between multiple AmazonVPCs, using VPC interface endpoints and VPC endpoint services.

Internal user connectivity options for Amazon VPC

- VPN for remote access software - In addition to network connection options for clients with Amazon VPC to connect remote users to VPC resources, this section describes how to use a remote access solution to provide end-users VPN access to an Amazon VPC.

Network connection with Amazon VPC

In this section, you will find design patterns that will enable you to link external networks to your Amazon VPC environment. These options are useful for integrating AWS tools with your existing on-premises services (such as tracking, authentication, protection, data, or other systems) by expanding your internal AWS Cloud networks. With this network extension, your internal users can also connect seamlessly to resources hosted on AWS, just like any other internal resource.

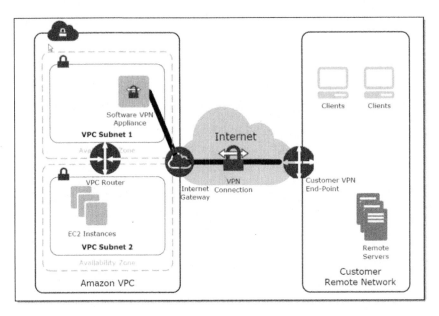

VPN managed by AWS

Amazon VPC provides the ability to establish an IPsec VPN connection between remote client networks and their Amazon VPC on the Internet, as shown in the following figure. Consider this method if you want to take advantage of an AWS-managed VPN endpoint with automatic redundancy and fallover of multiple data centers combined on the VPN connection's AWS side. Irrespective of the obscurity, two different VPN endpoints serve the Amazon Virtual Private Gateway, which are physically located in separate data centres to increase the availability of your VPN connection.

The Virtual Private Gateway also support and facilitate connections to multiple user gateways, so that, as shown in the following figure, you can enforce redundancy and fallover on your side of the VPN link. To provide flexibility in your routing setup, dynamic and static routing options are offered. To share routing information between AWS and these remote endpoints, dynamic routing uses BGP peering. Dynamic routing also allows you to specify routing priorities, policies, and weights (metrics) in your BGP ads and may also affect the path between your networks and AWS.

It is important to note that when using BGP, both IPSec and BGP connections must terminate on the same computer as the user gateway, hence both IPSec and BGP connections must be terminated.

AWS Direct Connection

AWS Direct Connect makes it possible for a local network and Amazon VPC to create a dedicated link. You can setup a private connection between your data centre and AWS, office or colocation area with the AWS Direct Connect. This private link will minimize network costs, improve bandwidth throughput, and provide a network experience more reliable than other Internet connections.

AWS Direct Connect allows you to establish dedicated 1 Gbps or 10 Gbps network connections (or multiple connections) between AWS networks and any of the AWS Direct Connect locations. It uses standard VLANs to access Amazon Elastic Compute Cloud (Amazon EC2) instances running on an Amazon VPC using private IP addresses. You can select from an ecosystem of WAN service providers to integrate your AWS Direct Connect endpoint into an AWS Direct Connect site with your external networks. The following figure illustrates this model. You can also work with your carrier to create a sub-1G connection or use a link aggregation group (LAG) to group multiple 1 gigabit or 10-gigabit connections together on a single AWS Direct Connect endpoint so you can handle them as one unified connection.

AWS Direct Connect + VPN

AWS Direct Connect + VPN allows you to combine one or more dedicated AWS Direct Connect network connections with Amazon VPC VPN. This combination provides an IPsec encrypted private connection that also lower network costs, increases bandwidth throughput, and provides a more consistent network experience than Internet-based VPN connections.

To establish a dedicated network link between your network, you can use AWS Direct Connect and establish a logical connection to AWS public resources, such as an IPsec endpoint for the Amazon virtual private gateway. This approach incorporates the low latency, higher bandwidth, more reliable benefits of the AWS Direct Connect approach and an end-to-end safe IPsec link with the AWS-managed advantages of the VPN solution.

This option is illustrated by the below image

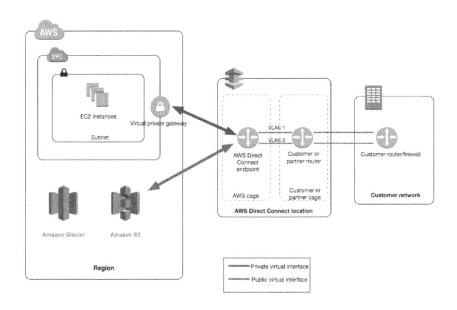

AWS VPN CloudHub

Based on the AWS Managed VPN and AWS Direct Connect options described earlier, you can communicate securely from one site to another using AWS VPN CloudHub. AWS VPN CloudHub works on a simple star model that you can use with or without VPC. Use this design if you have multiple branches and existing Internet connections and want to implement a practical and potentially cost-effective star model for primary or backup connections between these remote offices.

The image below illustrates the AWS VPN CloudHub architecture, with dashed blue lines indicating the network traffic between remote sites routed through their AWS VPN connections.

AWS VPN CloudHub manages an Amazon VPC virtual private gateway with multiple gateways and each uses unique BGP Autonomous System Numbers (ASNs). Your gateways will promote the correct routes (BGP prefixes) through their VPN connections.

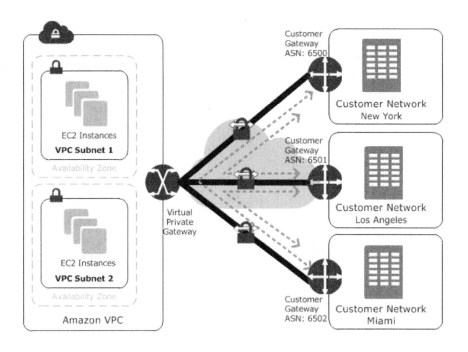

Software VPN

Amazon VPC gives you the flexibility to fully control both sides of your Amazon VPC connectivity by establishing a VPN connection between your remote network and a software VPN device running on your Amazon VPC network.

This option is recommended if you need to manage both ends of the VPN connection for compliance or if you want to use gateway devices that are currently not supported by the Amazon VPC VPN solution. The following figure illustrates this option.

You can choose from an ecosystem of various partners and open source communities that have produced software VPN devices running on Amazon EC2. These include products from well-known security companies such as Check Point, Astaro, OpenVPN Technologies and Microsoft, as well as popular open-source tools such as OpenVPN, Openswan and IPsec-Tools. This choice includes responsibility for managing the software device, focusing on configuration, patches, and upgrades.

Note that this design introduces a possible single point of failure in the network design, as the software VPN device runs on one Amazon EC2 instance.

Exam Essentials

- Understand the concept of a VPC, its key and optional elements. An Amazon VPC consists of the following basic elements: subnets (public, private and VPN only), route tables, DHCP option sets, security groups, and network

ACLs. Optional items include an IGW, EIP addresses, endpoints, peering connections, NAT instances, VPGs, CGWs and VPN connections.

- Understand the purpose of a subnet. A subnet is a segment of the Amazon VPC IP address range in which you can place groups of isolated resources. Subnets are defined by CIDR blocks (for example, 10.0.1.0/24 and 10.0.2.0/24) and are located in an availability area.
- Identify the distinction between a public subnet, a private subnet and a subnet-only VPN. When traffic is routed from a subnet to an IGW, the subnet is referred to as a public subnet. If a subnet has no route to the IGW, the subnet is called a private subnet. If a subnet has no route to the IGW, but the traffic is forwarded to a VPG, the subnet is referred to as a VPN-only subnet.
- Understand the purpose of a routing table. The routing table is a set of rules (called routes) that is used to determine where network traffic is directed. A routing table allows Amazon EC2 instances in different subnets to communicate with each other (within the same Amazon VPC).
- Understand what DHCP option sets provide for an Amazon VPC. Using the DHCP option sets element of an Amazon VPC, you can direct the Amazon EC2 hostname mapping to your resources. You can enter an instance domain name into an Amazon VPC and mark the IP addresses of custom DNS, NTP, and NetBIOS servers.
- Understand the difference between a public IP address for an Amazon VPC and an EIP address. A public IP address is an AWS IP address that can be allocated to instances that are automatically created on a subnet. An EIP address is an AWS public IP address that you assign to your account and to instances or network interfaces upon request.

- Understand what endpoints can offer an Amazon VPC. With an Amazon VPC endpoint, you can establish a private connection between your Amazon VPC and another AWS service without requiring access from the Internet or through a NAT instance, VPN connection, or AWS Direct Connect. The terminals only support services in the region.

- Understand Amazon VPC Peering. An Amazon VPC peering connection is a network connection between two Amazon VPCs that allow instances of both Amazon VPCs to communicate with each other as if they were on similar network. Furthermore, via a request / accept protocol, peer connections are created. Transitive peering is not allowed, and within the same region, peering is only possible between Amazon VPCs.

- Know the difference between a network ACL and a security community. The instance-level refers to a protection category. In many subnets that are part of the same protection classes, you may have several instances. Protection classes are stateful, which ensures that irrespective of outbound laws, return traffic is permitted automatically. A network ACL is applied at the subnet level, and the traffic remains stateless. You should allow inbound and outbound traffic on the network ACL so that Amazon EC2 instances on a subnet can communicate using a specific protocol.

- Understand what a NAT offers for an Amazon VPC. A NAT instance or NAT gateway allows instances in a private subnet to initiate outbound traffic to the Internet. This allows outbound Internet communications to download patches and updates. However, it prevents instances from receiving inbound traffic initiated by someone on the Internet.

- To create a VPN link from a network to an Amazon VPC, understand the components needed. A VPG is the VPN concentrator between the two networks on the AWS side of

119

the VPN connection. The VPN connection must be established on the CGW side, and this connection consists of two IPSec tunnels.

Review Questions

1. What is the range of permitted IPv4 prefix lengths for a VPC CIDR block?

A. /16 to /28

B. /16 to /56

C. /8 to /30

D. /56 only

2. You've created a VPC with the CIDR 192.168.16.0/24. You want to assign a secondary CIDR to this VPC. Which CIDR can you use?

A. 172.31.0.0/16

B. 192.168.0.0/16

C. 192.168.0.0/24

D. 192.168.16.0/23

3. You need to create two subnets in a VPC that has a CIDR of 10.0.0.0/16. Which of the following CIDRs can you assign to one of the subnets while leaving room for an additional subnet? (Choose all that apply.)

A. 10.0.0.0/24

B. 10.0.0.0/8

C. 10.0.0.0/16

D. 10.0.0.0/23

4. What is the minimum subnet size you can have in an Amazon VPC?

A. / 24

B. / 26

C. / 28

D. / 30

5. You made a new subnet and then added a route that uses an IGW to route traffic from that subnet to the Internet and to your routing table. What kind of subnet have you built?

A. An internal subnet

B. A private subnet with a private net

C. An External Subnet

D. A subnet for the public

6. When you create a new Amazon VPC, what happens?

A. By default, the main route table is generated.

B. By default, three subnets are established, one for every Availability Region.

C. Three subnets are created by default in an availability zone.

D. An IGW is created by default.

7. In East US 1, you built a new VPC and added three subnets in that Amazon VPC. Which of the following statements is true?

A. These subnets are not capable of communicating with each other by default; you need to build routes.

B. By default, every subnet is public.

C. Both subnets can communicate by default with each other.

D. Each subnet has similar CIDR blocks.

8. How many IGWs can you connect to an Amazon VPC at the same time?

A. 1

B. 2

C. 3

D. 4

9. What is a stateful feature of an Amazon VPC?

A. ACL network

B. Groups of defence

C. DynamoDB Amazon

D. The S3 Amazon

10. With private and public subnets, you have created a custom Amazon VPC. You have a NAT instance generated, and this instance is deployed on a public subnet. You've added an EIP address to the routing table and also added your NAT. Unfortunately, the Internet is still unreachable by instances in your private subnet. What could be the cause?

A. Your NAT is on a public subnet but must be on a private subnet.

B. Your NAT must be behind an Elastic Load Balancer.

C. You must disable source/destination controls for NAT.

D. Your NAT is deployed on a Windows instance, but your other instances are Linux. It would help if you redeployed NAT on a Linux instance.

11. When an Amazon EC2 instance sponsored by Amazon Elastic Block Store (Amazon EBS) in an Amazon VPC with an associated EIP is halted and restarted, which of the following events will occur? (Choose 2 answers).

A. The EIP will be disconnected from the procedure.

B. All data on the instance storage devices will be destroyed.

C. All the data on Amazon EBS computers will be lost.

D. ENI remains Freestanding.

E. The host child of the case becomes shifted.

12. How many VPC peering links for four VPCs located in the same AWS area are required to send traffic to others?

A.3

B. 4

C. 5

D. 6

13. 13. To resolve DNS names outside of AWS, which of the following AWS tools will you use to acquire an EC2 VPC instance?

A. A VPC peering connection

B. A set of DHCP options

C. A routing rule

D. An IGW

14. Which of the following is the Amazon side connected to an Amazon VPN?

A. An EIP

B. A CGW

C. An IGW

D. A VPG

15. What is the default limit for the number of Amazon VPCs that a client may have in an area?

A. 5

B. 6

C. 7

D. There is no maximum limit for VPCs available within a region by design.

Answer to Review Questions

1. A. The allowed range of prefix lengths for a VPC CIDR is between /16 and /28 inclusive. The maximum possible prefix length for an IP subnet is /32, hence, /56 is not a valid length.

2. C. A secondary CIDR may come from similar RFC 1918 address range as the primary option, but it may not overlap the primary CIDR. 192.168.0.0/24 comes from the same address range (192.168.0.0–192.168.255.255) as the primary option and does not overlap with 192.168.16.0/24. 192.168.0.0/16 and 192.168.16.0/23 both overlap with 192.168.16.0/24. 172.31.0.0/16 is not in the same range as the primary CIDR.

3. A, D. 10.0.0.0/24 and 10.0.0.0/23 are within the VPC CIDR and they leave room for a second subnet. 10.0.0.0/8 is wrong because prefix lengths less than /16 aren't allowed. 10.0.0.0/16 doesn't leave room for another subnet.

4. A. The maximum subnet size you can have in a VPC is / 16.

5. D. By creating a route to the Internet using an IGW, you have made this subnet public.

6. A. When you create an Amazon VPC, a route table is created by default. It would be helpful if you manually created subnets and an IGW.

7. C. When you set up an Amazon VPC, all subnets can communicate by default.

8. A. You can only have one IGW for each Amazon VPC.

9. B. Security groups are stateful, while network ACLs are stateless.

10. C. You must disable source/destination checks for NAT.

11. B, E. In the EC2-Classic network, the EIP is disconnected from the instance; in the EC2-VPC network, the EIP remains connected to the instance. The stop/start option of an Amazon EBS-based Amazon EC2 instance always changes the host computer regardless of the underlying network.

12. D. Six VPC peering connections are required for each of the four VPCs to send traffic to each other.

13. B. With a set of DHCP options, clients can define DNS servers for DNS name resolution, set domain names for instances within an Amazon VPC, define NTP servers, and define the NetBIOS name servers.

14. D. A CGW is the client side of a VPN connection and a network is linked to the Internet by an IGW. The Amazon side of a VPN connection is a VPG.

15. A. The default limit on the number of Amazon VPCs a customer can have in a region is 5.

Chapter 4

Database

A database helps an application store, organize, and easily retrieve data. While you might use flat files to store data, as the number of data increases, they become increasingly slow to scan. By relying on database to perform these tasks, developers are free to focus on the application without having to directly interact with a file system to store and retrieve data.

Consequently, the availability and performance of a database-backed application depend on the database you choose and its configuration. Databases come in two forms: relational and non-relational. Each of these differs in the way it stores, organizes, and lets you retrieve data. Hence, the type of database you choose depends on the needs of the application.

In this chapter, you'll learn the differences between these two database types and how to select the right one for your application. You'll also learn how to use the managed database services that AWS provides to get the level of performance and reliability your applications require, as well as how to protect your data and recover it in the event of a database failure.

This chapter will introduce three different managed database services provided by AWS.

- Relational database service (RDS)

- Redshift
- DynamoDB

Relational Databases

A relational database contains at least one table, which you can visualize as a spreadsheet with columns and rows. In a relational database table, columns may also be termed attributes, and rows may also be termed records or tuples.

Columns and Attributes

Before you can add data to a relational database table, you must predefine each column's name and what data types it can accept. Columns are ordered, and you can't change the order after creating the table. The ordering creates a relationship between attributes on the table, and this is where the term relational database emanates from.

Using Multiple Tables

Storing all data in a single table can lead to unnecessary duplication, needlessly increasing the size of the database and making queries slower. Hence, it's common for applications to use multiple related tables. Using the preceding example, if 50 employees work in the information technology department, the string "Information technology" appears in the table 50 times—once for each record. To avoid this space wastage, you may create a separate table to hold department names.

Structured Query Language

The Structured Query Language (SQL) with relational databases is used to store and query data and to also perform database maintenance tasks. For this reason, relational databases are often called SQL databases.

SQL statements differ slightly depending on the specific relational database management system (RDBMS) you're using. As an AWS architect, you don't need to totally understand SQL, as all major programming languages have libraries that construct SQL statements and interact with the database. However, when dealing with AWS-managed database offerings, you need to understand the concepts behind a few common SQL terms.

Querying Data

To query data from a SQL database, the SELECT statement is applied. This allows you to query based on the value in any column, and also to define the unique columns which you would like to return to the database. Thanks to the predictable structure of tables and the enforcement of foreign key constraints, you can use a JOIN clause with a SELECT statement to combine data from different tables.

Storing Data

The INSERT statement enables you to explicitly insert data into a table. You may use the COPY command to copy data from a correctly formatted file to the table you define if you need to load a large number of documents.

Online Transaction Processing vs. Online Analytic Processing

A relational database can fall, depending on its configuration, into one of the two categories:

- Online transaction processing (OLTP)
- Online analytical processing (OLAP).

- OLTP

OLTP databases are suitable for applications that read and write data frequently, on the order of multiple times per second. For fast searches, they are configured, and these searches are generally routine and predictable. The size of the database and the performance criteria are dependent on certain criteria. An OLTP database can possess high memory requirements, so it can store frequently used parts of tables in memory for quick access.

- OLAP

OLAP databases are optimized for complex queries on large data sets. As a result, OLAP databases typically have significant compute and storage requirements. In data warehousing applications, it is common to merge multiple OLTP databases into one OLAP database.

Amazon Relational Database Service

The Relational Database Service (RDS) from Amazon is a managed database service that allows you to run cloud-based relational database systems. RDS takes care of the configuration of the storage infrastructure, carry out backups, maintain high availability, and restores the software and operating system of the underlying database. RDS also makes it easy to restore, recover data and scale your databases from database failures in order to reach the level of performance and availability proposed for your application.

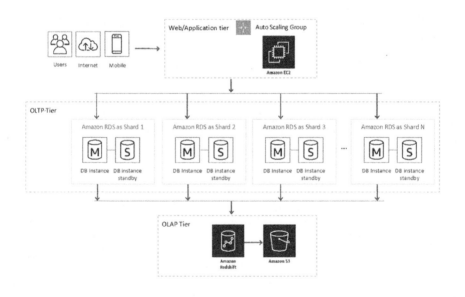

Engines Database

The program that stores, organizes and retrieves data in a database is simply a database engine. A single DB Engine runs each DB case. RDS offers the following six database engines:

MySQL MySQL is optimized for OLTP applications, including e-commerce and blogs. RDS offers the latest MySQL Community Edition versions, including 5.5, 5.6, and 5.7. MySQL offers two storage engines—MyISAM and InnoDB—but the latter should be used as it's the only type compatible with RDS-managed automatic backups.

For MySQL, MariaDB is a drop-in binary substitute. After Oracle bought the firm that built it originally, it was created due to fears surrounding MySQL 's future. RDS offers many versions of MariaDB, ranging from 10.0.17 through 10.2. MariaDB supports the XtraDB and InnoDB storage engines, but AWS recommends using the latter to ensure maximum compatibility with RDS.

Oracle is one of the most generally used relational database management systems. Some applications specifically need an Oracle database. RDS provides the following

Oracle Database editions:

- Standard Edition One (SE1)
- Standard Edition Two (SE2)
- Standard Edition (SE)
- Enterprise Edition (EE)

PostgreSQL advertises itself as the open source database that is most compliant with Oracle. This is a good choice to consider when you have in-house applications that were developed for Oracle but want to minimize costs. RDS offers versions of PostgreSQL ranging from 9.3.12-R1 through 10.4-R1.

For MySQL and PostgreSQL, Amazon Aurora is Amazon's drop-in binary replacement. By utilizing a virtualized storage layer which decreases the number of rights to the underlying storage, Aurora provides better writing efficiency than both. It provides three editions.

- MySQL 5.6-compatible
- MySQL 5.7-compatible
- PostgreSQL compatible

Microsoft SQL Server RDS offers multiple Microsoft SQL Server versions: 2008 R2, 2012, 2014, 2016, and 2017. For the edition, you can choose Express, Web, Standard, and Enterprise. The selection of any of these options allow an existing SQL Server database to be migrated from an on-prem implementation to RDS without requiring any database updates to be performed.

Considerations on Licensing

RDS supports two models for licensing the database engine program you are running. The model included with the license covers the expense of the license for an RDS, especially for the pricing. The BYOL model allows you to obtain a license for the database engine you're running.

License Included MariaDB and MySQL uses the GNU General Public License (GPL) v2.0, and PostgreSQL uses the PostgreSQL license, all of which allow free usage of the respective software.

All Microsoft SQL Server versions and editions you run on RDS require a license, as do Oracle Database Standard Edition One (SE1) and Standard Edition Two (SE2).

The following Oracle Database editions allow you to forward your license:

- Enterprise Edition (EE)
- Standard Edition (SE)
- Standard Edition One (SE1)
- Standard Edition Two (SE2)

Database Option Groups

Database engines offer various features to help you manage your databases and improve security. Option groups allows you specify these features—called options—and apply them to one or more instances. Options require more memory, hence, make sure your instances have ample memory and enable only the options you need.

Database Instance Classes

When launching a database instance, you must decide how much processing power, memory, network bandwidth, and disk throughput it requires. RDS offers a variety of database instance classes to meet the diverse performance needs of different databases. If you get it wrong or if it requires change, you can switch your instance to a different class. RDS divides database instance classes into the following three types.

Standard

Standard instance classes meet the needs of most databases. The latest-generation instance class is db.m4, which provides up to:

- 256 GB memory
- 64 vCPU
- 25 Gbps network bandwidth
- 10,000 Mbps (1,280 MBps) disk throughput

Memory-Optimized

Memory-optimized instance classes are for databases that have hefty performance requirements. Creating more memory for a database allows it to store more data and this can result in faster query times. The latest-generation instance class is db.x1e, and it provides up to:

- 3,904 GB memory
- 128 vCPU
- 25 Gbps network bandwidth
- 14,000 Mbps (1,750 MBps) disk throughput

Instances in a database uses the EBS storage. EBS-optimized are both regular and memory-optimized instance class types, meaning they have dedicated bandwidth for transfers from and to EBS storage.

Burst Capable (Burstable)

Burstable instances are developed for development, test, and other nonproduction databases. The only burstable instance class available is db.t2, and it gives you up to:

- 32 GB memory
- 8 vCPU

AWS indicates that the network performance is "moderate," which in most cases, corresponds to less than 1 Gbps. AWS doesn't provide stats on disk throughput, but you shouldn't expect to obtain more than 3,200 Mbps (400 MBps).

Whether you implement a relational or non-relational database depends solely on the application which will apply it. Relational databases have been in town for a long time, and many application developers default to modeling their data to fit into a relational database. Applications use database-specific SDKs to interact with the database, and therefore, the needs of the application mandate the specific database engine required. This is why AWS RDS offers six of the most popular database engines and sports compatibility with a wide range of versions. The idea is to let you take an existing database and port it to RDS without the application requiring any further adjustments.

Exam Essentials

- Understand the differences between relational and non-relational databases. A relational database requires you to specify attributes upfront when creating a table. All data you insert into a table must fit into the predefined attributes. It uses the Structured Query Language (SQL) to read and write data, and so it's also called a SQL database. A non-relational database only requires you to specify a primary key attribute when creating a table. All items in a table must include a primary key but can otherwise have different attributes. Nonrelational—also called no-SQL databases—store unstructured data.

- Know the different database engines RDS supports. RDS supports all of the most popular database engines—MySQL, MariaDB, Oracle, PostgreSQL, Amazon Aurora, and Microsoft SQL Server. Understand the difference between the bring-your-own-license and license-included licensing models. Know which database engines support which licensing models.

- Be able to select the right instance class and storage type, given specific storage requirements. Memory and storage tend to be the constraining factors for relational databases, so you must know how to choose the right instance class and storage type based on the performance needs of a database. Know the three different instance classes: standard, memory-optimized, and burstable. Furthermore, be familiar with how these relate to the three different storage types: general-purpose SSD (gp2), provisioned IOPS SSD (io1), and magnetic.

- Understand the differences between multi-AZ and read replicas. Both multi-AZ and read replicas involve creating additional database instances, but there are some key

138

differences. A read replica can service queries, while a standby instance in a multi-AZ deployment cannot. A master instance asynchronously replicates data to read replicas, while in a multi-AZ configuration, the primary instance synchronously replicates data to the standby. Understand how Aurora replicas different work and how Aurora multi-AZ differs from multi-AZ of other database engines.

- Determine the appropriate primary key type for a DynamoDB table. DynamoDB tables give you two options for a primary key. A simple primary key consists of just a partition key and a single value. DynamoDB distribute items across partitions based on the value of the partition key. When using a simple primary key, the partition key must be unique within a table. A primary composite key consists of a partition key and a key for sorting. The partition key does not have to be unique, but it must be a combination of the partition key and the sort key.

- Know how DynamoDB throughput capacity works. When you create a table, you must specify throughput capacity to write and read capacity units. The read capacity units a read consumes depends on two things: whether the read is strongly or eventually consistent and how much data you read within one second. For an item of up to 4 KB in size, one strongly consistent read consumes one read capacity unit. Eventually, consistent reads consume half of that. When it comes to writes, one write capacity unit lets you write up to one 1 KB item per second.

Review Questions

1. In a relational database, a row may also be called what? (Choose two.)

A. Record

B. Attribute

C. Tuple

D. Table

2. What must every relational database table contain?

A. A foreign key

B. A primary key

C. An attribute

D. A row

3. Which SQL statement would you use to retrieve data from a relational database table?

A. QUERY

B. SCAN

C. INSERT

D. SELECT

4. Which relational database type is optimized to handle multiple transactions per second?

A. Offline transaction processing (OLTP)

B. Online transaction processing (OLTP)

C. Online analytic processing (OLAP)

D. Key-value store

5. How many database engines can a RDS database instance run?

A. Six

B. One

C. Two

D. Four

6. Which database engines are compatible with existing MySQL databases? (Choose all options that apply.)

A. Microsoft SQL Server

B. MariaDB

C. Aurora

D. PostgreSQL

7. Which storage engine can you use with MySQL, Aurora, and MariaDB for maximum compatibility with RDS?

A. MyISAM

B. XtraDB

C. InnoDB

D. PostgreSQL

8. Which database engine supports the bring-your-own-license (BYOL) model? (Choose all options that apply.)

A. Oracle Standard Edition Two

B. Microsoft SQL Server

C. Oracle Standard Edition One

D. PostgreSQL

9. Which database instance class provides dedicated bandwidth for storage volumes?

A. Standard

B. Memory-optimized

C. Storage optimized

D. Burstable

10. If a MariaDB database running in RDS needs to write 200 MB of data every second, how many IOPS should you apply for io1 storage to sustain this performance?

A. 12,800

B. 25,600

C. 200

D. 16

11. Using general-purpose SSD storage, how much storage would you need to allocate to get 600 IOPS?

A. 200 GB

B. 100 GB

C. 200 TB

D. 200 MB

12. If you need to achieve 12,000 IOPS using provisioned IOPS SSD storage, how much storage should you allocate, assuming that you need only 100 GB of storage?

A. There is no minimum storage requirement.

B. 200 GB

C. 240 GB

D. 12 TB

13. What type of database instance only accepts queries?

A. Read replica

B. Standby database instance

C. Primary database instance

D. Master database instance

14. In a multi-AZ deployment using Oracle, how is data replicated?

A. Synchronously from the primary instance to a read replica

B. Synchronously using a cluster volume

C. Asynchronously from the primary to a standby instance

D. Synchronously from the primary to a standby instance

15. Which of the following occurs when you restore a failed database instance from a snapshot?

A. RDS restores the snapshot to a new instance.

B. RDS restores the snapshot to the failed instance.

C. RDS restores only the individual databases to a new instance.

D. RDS deletes the snapshot.

Answer to Review Questions

1. A, C. Different relational databases use different terminologies. A row, record, and tuple all describe an ordered set of columns. An attribute is another term for the column. A table contains rows and columns.

144

2. C. A table must contain at least one attribute or column. Primary and foreign keys are used for relating data in different tables, but they're not required. A row can exist within a table, but a table doesn't need a row to exist.

3. D. The SELECT statement retrieves data from a table. INSERT is used for adding data to a table. QUERY and SCAN are commands used by DynamoDB, which is a non-relational database.

4. B. Online transaction processing databases are designed to handle multiple transactions per second. Online analytics processing databases are used for complex queries against large data sets. A key-value store such as DynamoDB can handle multiple transactions per second, but it's not a relational database. There's no such thing as an offline transaction processing database.

5. B. Although there are six database engines to choose from, a single database instance can run only one database engine. You will require a different instance of the database for each engine if you want to run more than one database engine.

6. B, C. MariaDB and Aurora are designed as binary drop-in replacements for MySQL. PostgreSQL is designed for compatibility with Oracle databases. Microsoft SQL Server does not support MySQL databases.

7. C. InnoDB is the only storage engine Amazon recommends for MySQL and MariaDB deployments in RDS and the only engine Aurora supports. MyISAM is another storage engine that works with MySQL but it is not compatible with automated backups. XtraDB is another storage engine for MariaDB, but Amazon no longer recommends it. The PostgreSQL database engine uses its own storage engine by the same name and it is not compatible with other database engines.

8. A, C. All editions of the Oracle database engine support the bring-your-own-license model in RDS. Microsoft SQL Server and PostgreSQL only supports the license included model.

9. B. Memory-optimized instances are EBS optimized, providing dedicated bandwidth for EBS storage. Standard instances are not EBS optimized and further tops at 10,000 Mbps disk throughput. Burstable (burst capable) instances are designed for development and test workloads and provide the lowest disk throughput of any instance class. Furthermore, no instance class is called storage optimized.

10. A. MariaDB has a page size of 16 KB. To write 200 MB (204,800 KB) of data every second, it would require 12,800 IOPS. Oracle, PostgreSQL, or Microsoft SQL Server will use an 8 KB page size and would need 25,600 IOPS to achieve the same throughput. When provisioning IOPS, you must specify IOPS in increments of 1,000, so 200 and 16 IOPS—which would be woefully insufficient anyway—are not valid answers.

11. A. General-purpose SSD storage allocates three IOPS per gigabyte, up to 10,000 IOPS. Therefore, to attain 600 IOPS, you'd need to allocate 200 GB. Allocating 100 GB would only give you 300 IOPS. The maximum storage size for gp2 storage is 16 TB, so 200 TB is not a valid value. The minimum amount of storage you can allocate depends on the database engine, but it's no less than 20 GB, hence, 200 MB is not valid.

12. C. When you install IOPS using io1 storage, you must do so in a ratio no greater than 50 IOPS for 1 GB. Allocating 240 GB of storage would give you 12,000 IOPS. Allocating 200 GB of storage would fall short, yielding just 10,000 IOPS. Allocating 12 TB would be an overkill for the amount of storage required.

13. A. A read replica only services queries and cannot write on a database. A standby database instance in a multi-AZ deployment does not accept queries. Both a primary and master database instance can service both queries and writes.

14. D. Multi-AZ deployments using Oracle, PostgreSQL, MariaDB, MySQL, or Microsoft SQL Server replicate data synchronously from the primary to a standby instance. Only a multi-AZ deployment using Aurora uses a cluster volume and replicates data to a specific type of reading replica called an Aurora replica.

15. A. When you restore from a snapshot, RDS creates a new instance and doesn't make any changes to the failed instance. A snapshot is a copy of the entire instance, not just a copy of the

individual databases. RDS does not delete a snapshot after restoring from it.

Chapter 5

AWS Risk and Compliance

This chapter provides information to help customers integrate AWS into their existing control framework, including a basic approach for evaluating AWS controls.

AWS and its customers share control of the computing environment. Part of this shared responsibility of AWS includes providing its services on a highly secured and monitored platform and providing a wide variety of security features for customers to use. The customer's responsibility includes configuring their IT environments in a secured and controlled manner for their purposes. While customers do not communicate their uses and configurations to AWS, AWS does communicate the relevant security and control environment to customers. AWS does this by taking the following steps:

- Obtain industrial certifications and independent external attestations as described in this document
- Publish information about AWS security and auditing practices in white papers and website content
- Provide certificates, reports and other documents directly to AWS customers under NDA (if required)

Shared Responsibility Environment

The transition from IT infrastructure to AWS services create a model of shared responsibility between customer and AWS. As AWS runs, manages and monitors components from the host operating system and from the virtualization layer to the physical protection of the facilities where the service runs, this shared model will help reduce the operational burden for the client. The guest operating system (including updates and security patches), other related application software, and the configuration of the security group firewall supported by AWS are responsible for and operated by the customer.

As their roles differ depending on the services used, the incorporation of those services into their IT environment, and relevant laws and regulations, clients should carefully consider the services they choose. By leveraging technologies such as host-based firewalls, network-based host intrusion detection/prevention, encryption and key management, customers may enhance protection and/or meet more stringent enforcement requirements.

Flexibility and consumer control that allow solutions which meet industry-specific certification criteria to be introduced, often provide the essence of this shared responsibility.

This model of shared customer/AWS responsibility also extends to IT controls. Just as the responsibility for operating the IT environment is shared between AWS and its customers, the administration, execution and validation of IT controls are shared. By handling the controls associated with the physical infrastructure installed in the AWS setting that would have previously been handled by the customer, AWS may help the client ease the burden of operational controls.

Because every customer is deployed differently in AWS, customers can benefit from moving the management of some IT controls to

AWS, resulting in a (new) distributed control environment. Customers can then use the AWS monitoring and compliance documentation available to them (described in AWS certifications and third-party attestations) to conduct their required monitoring and verification review procedures.

Strong Compliance Management

As always, AWS customers are required to maintain adequate governance throughout the IT control environment, regardless of how IT is implemented. Best practices include understanding the objectives and required compliance requirements (from relevant sources), establishing a controlled environment that meets these objectives and requirements, understanding the required validation based on the organization's risk tolerance, and verifying the operational effectiveness of their control environment.

Deployment in the AWS Cloud offers companies several options to apply different types of controls and different authentication methods.

Strong customer compliance and governance can include the following basic approaches:

1. Review the information available on AWS along with other information to gain the greatest possible insight on the entire IT environment, then document all compliance requirements.
2. Design and implement audit objectives to meet business compliance requirements.
3. Identify and document third party audits.

4. Verify that all control objectives are in line and that all significant controls are designed and are operating effectively.

By approaching compliance governance in this manner, companies will better understand their control environment and be able to define the audit activities to be performed.

AWS Monitors Assessment and Integration

AWS provides a wide range of information about its IT control environment to customers through white papers, reports, certifications and other third party statements. This documentation helps customers understand the existing controls that are applicable to the AWS services they use and how they have checked those controls. This information also aid customers in their efforts to report and validate that the controls are working effectively in their comprehensive IT environment.

Traditionally, the design and operational effectiveness of audit objectives and controls are validated by internal and/or external auditors through step-by-step processes and evidence evaluation. Direct observation/verification, by the client or the client's external auditor, is usually performed to validate the controls. When using service providers such as AWS, businesses request and review third-party licenses and certifications in order to gain fair assurance as to the design and operational efficacy of the audit goals and controls. Therefore, while AWS can manage the client's core controls, the control environment can still be a unified framework in which all controls are viewed and verified as functioning effectively.

152

AWS attestations and third party certifications can not only provide a higher level of validation of the control environment but can also relieve customers of the obligation to ascertain some form of validation for their IT environment in the AWS cloud.

AWS IT control information

AWS delivers IT control information to customers in the following ways:

Definition of specific control.

AWS customers can identify the key controls managed by AWS. Key controls are essential to the customer's control environment and require external certification of the operational effectiveness of these key controls to meet compliance requirements, such as the annual financial audit. To this end, AWS publishes a wide variety of specific IT controls in its service organization.

Control report 1 (SOC 1) Type II.

The SOC 1 report, formerly the Service Organizations Report Statement on Auditing Standards (SAS) No. 70, is a commonly accepted auditing standard established by the American Institute of Certified Public Accountants. The SOC 1 audit is an inner audit of the design, and operational effectiveness of the AWS identified control objectives and control activities (including control objectives and control activities on the part of the AWS controlled infrastructure). 'Type II' refers to the fact that each of the controls mentioned in the report is not only checked by the external auditor for design adequacy but also evaluated for operational performance. Due to the independence and integrity of the external auditor of AWS, the controls defined in the report must give clients a high degree of trust in the AWS control environment.

AWS audits are designed and created to function effectively for many compliance purposes, including Sarbanes-Oxley (SOX) Section 404 audits of financial statements. The use of SOC 1 Type II reports as generally permitted by other third-party certification authorities (for example, ISO 27001 auditors can request a SOC 1 Type II report to complete their customer reviews).

Other specific monitoring activities are related to payment card industry (PCI) compliance with AWS and the Federal Information Security Management Act (FISMA). AWS complies with FISMA Moderate and PCI Data Security Standard. These PCI and FISMA standards are highly prescriptive and requires independent validation for AWS to comply with the published standard.

Compliance with General Auditing Standards.

If an AWS customer needs a broad set of audit goals to be met, an assessment of the AWS industry certifications can be performed. With AWS ISO 27001 certification, AWS adheres to a broad and comprehensive security standard and follows best practices to maintain a secured environment. Along with the PCI Data Security Standard (PCI DSS), AWS meets a series of key controls for businesses managing credit card information. As AWS is FISMA compliant, AWS complies with a wide variety of specific controls required by the US government agencies. Adhering to these global standards provide customers with detailed information about the general nature of the security controls and processes in place, which can be taken into account when managing compliance.

AWS Global Regions

Data centres are built in clusters in different regions of the world, including US East (N. Virginia), US West (Oregon), US West (Northern California), AWS GovCloud (US) (Oregon), EU (Frankfurt), EU (Ireland)), Asia-Pacific (Seoul), Asia-Pacific (Singapore), Asia-Pacific (Tokyo), Asia-Pacific (Sydney), China (Beijing), and South America (Sao Paulo).

AWS Risk and Compliance Program

AWS provides information about its risk management and compliance program to enable customers integrate AWS controls into their governance framework. With AWS as an integral part of the process, this knowledge will help clients document a robust governance and control structure.

Risk Management

AWS management has established a proactive business strategy that requires the detection of threats and the implementation of risk reduction or management controls. AWS management reassesses the strategic business plan at least twice a year. This process requires management to identify risks in its areas of responsibility and implement appropriate measures to address those risks.

Moreover, the monitoring environment of the AWS is subject to different internal and external risk assessments. AWS Compliance and Management teams have developed an information security policy and policies focused on the Information and Associated Technology Control Objectives (COBIT) policy and have effectively implemented the ISO 27001 certifiable framework based on ISO 27002 audits, Trust Services Standards of the American Institute of Certified Public Accountants (AICPA), PCI DSS v3.1 and National Institute v3.1 Information from the federal). AWS enforces security policies, provides staff with security training and conduct tests of application security. These assessments analyze data protection, honesty and availability, as well as compliance with policies on information security.

AWS Security periodically scans all IP addresses of Internet service endpoints for vulnerabilities (these scans do not include client instances). AWS Security notifies the appropriate parties to fix identified vulnerabilities. In addition, external threat analysis are regularly performed by independent security companies. The conclusions and recommendations resulting from these assessments are categorized and forwarded to AWS management. These scans are performed to ensure the integrity and viability of the underlying

AWS infrastructure and are not intended to replace the customer vulnerability scans needed to meet their specific compliance requirements.

Control Management

AWS maintains a robust control environment that involves policies, procedures, and activities of control that exploit different facets of the overall Amazon control environment. For safe delivery of AWS service offerings, this controlled environment is put in place. The collective control environment includes the individuals, procedures, and technologies required to build and sustain an environment that supports the AWS control framework's operational effectiveness. AWS has included applicable cloud-specific controls identified by leading organizations in the cloud computing industry as part of the AWS Control Framework. AWS continues to follow these industry groups for ideas relating to industry-leading practices that can be implemented to help customers better manage their control environment.

Amazon's control environment begins at the top level of the company. Leadership and senior management play an important role in setting the tone and core values of the company. Each employee receives the company's code of conduct and ethics and takes periodic training courses. Compliance audits are conducted so that employees understand and follow established policies.

The AWS organizational structure provides a system for organizing, conducting, and managing business activities. To ensure adequate staffing, effective operations and segregation of duties, the organizational structure assigns roles and responsibilities. Management has also established the appropriate authority and reporting lines for key personnel. The company's hiring verification processes include training, prior employment, and in some cases, background checks, as permitted by law and regulation, for employees and this is based on the company's position, employee level and level of access to AWS facilities.

Information Security

To protect the integrity, confidentiality, and availability of customer systems and data, AWS has introduced a structured information security policy. AWS publishes a security whitepaper on its public website explaining how AWS can help customers keep their data secured.

AWS Contact

Customers may submit reports and certifications prepared by our third-party auditors or by contacting AWS Sales and Business Development to submit more information on AWS compliance. The representative will refer customers to the appropriate team based on the nature of the investigation. For more information on AWS compliance, visit the AWS Compliance site or send your questions directly to mailto: awscompliance@amazon.com.

Essential Exam

- Understand the shared responsibility model. The shared responsibility model is not limited to security considerations; it also extends to IT audits. For example, management, operation, and verification of IT controls are shared between AWS and the customer. AWS enforces these controls with respect to the physical infrastructure.
- Remember that IT governance is the responsibility of the customer. The customer is responsible for ensuring adequate management of the whole IT control setting, regardless of how the IT is deployed (on-premise, cloud or hybrid).
- Understand how AWS provides monitoring information. AWS delivers IT control information to customers in two ways: through a specific control definition and through compliance with more general control standards.
- Remember, AWS is very proactive when it comes to risk management. AWS takes risk management very seriously and has, therefore developed a business plan to identify risks and implement controls to mitigate or manage those risks. An AWS leadership team reassesses the corporate risk management plan at least twice a year.
- The management team members are expected to recognize risks in their respective areas of responsibility as part of this process and then enforce controls designed to resolve and perhaps even discard those risks.
- Remember that the control environment is not solely based on technology. Regulation, procedures and monitoring operations are included in the AWS control system. People, procedures and technologies are included in this control setting.
- Don't forget important reports, certifications and third-party attestations. Important third party reports, certifications and attestations include, but are not limited to, the following:
  - FedRAMP

159

- FIPS 140-2
- FISMA and DIACAP
- HIPAA
- ISO 9001
- ISO 27001
- ITAR
- PCI DSS level 1
- SOC 1 / ISAE 3402
- SOC 2
- SOC 3

Review Questions

1. AWS communicates with customers about its security and control environment through various mechanisms. Which of the following are valid mechanisms? (Choose 3 answers)

A. Obtain industrial certifications and independent third-party representations

B. Post information about AWS security and auditing practices through the website, white papers and blogs

C. Provide certificates, reports and other documents directly to customers (in some cases under NDA)

D. Provide customer auditors direct access to AWS data centres, infrastructure and senior management

2. Which of the following statements about the AWS Model of Shared Responsibility is true?

A. The paradigm of shared accountability is restricted to safety considerations; it does not extend to computer controllers.

B. The shared responsibility model only applies to customers that are willing to comply with the SOC 1 Type II.

C. The model of shared responsibility is not limited to security considerations; it also extends to IT audits.

D. The shared responsibility model only applies to customers who wish to comply with ISO 27001.

3. AWS delivers IT control information to customers in any of the following ways?

A. Using specific audit definitions or following common auditing standards

B. Use of specific audit definitions or through SAS 70

C. Compliance with general principles of auditing and in accordance with ISO 27001

D. By meeting the requirements of ISO 27001 and SOC 1 Type II

4. What is a valid third party report, certification or attestation for AWS? (Choose 3 answers)

A. SOC 1

B. PCI DSS level 1

C. SOC 4

D. ISO 27001

5. Which of the following statements is true?

A. IT governance is still the responsibility of the customer, despite the implementation of their IT infrastructure on the AWS platform.

B. The AWS platform is PCI DSS Level 1 compliant. Customers can deploy their web applications on this platform and will automatically be PCI DSS compliant.

C. The shared responsibility model applies only to IT security; it's not about governance.

D. AWS does not take risk management very seriously, and it is the customer's responsibility to mitigate risk to the AWS infrastructure.

6. Which of the following statements is true about the risks and compliance benefits of the AWS environment?

A. Workloads must be fully moved to the AWS Cloud to comply with various third-party certifications and attestations.

B. Critical components of a workload must be fully moved to the AWS Cloud to comply with various third-party certifications and attestations, but not non-critical components.

C. Non-critical components of a workload must be completely moved to the AWS Cloud to meet various third-party certifications and attestations, but critical components must not be moved.

D. Few, several, or all components of a workload may be transferred to the AWS Cloud, but the customer must ensure that their whole workload continues to comply with various certifications and certificates from third parties.

7. Which of the definitions better describes a zone of availability?

A. A single, distinct data centre with redundant power and network/connectivity consists of each availability zone.

B. Two discrete data centres with redundant power and network/connectivity consist of each availability region.

C. Each zone of availability consists of many distinct zones, each with redundant power and network/communication data centre.

D. Multiple distinct data centres with shared power and redundant network/connectivity consist of each availability region.

8. As for the AWS platform's vulnerability scanning and threat analysis, which of the following statements is true? (Choose 2 answers)

A. AWS regularly scans the IP addresses of publicly available endpoints for vulnerabilities.

B. Scans performed by AWS include customer instances.

C. AWS Security notifies the appropriate parties to fix identified vulnerabilities.

D. Customers may perform their own analysis at any time without notice.

9. Which of the following best describes customer risk communications and compliance responsibilities for AWS?

A. AWS and customers share information about their security and control environment at all times.

B. AWS publishes information about AWS security and auditing practices online and directly to customers under NDA. Customers do not need to report their usage and configurations to AWS.

C. Customers communicate their usage and configurations to AWS at all times. AWS does not communicate AWS security and auditing practices to customers for security reasons.

D. Customers and AWS retain their entirely proprietary protection and control procedures and do not disclose them to ensure the highest form of protection for both parties.

10. In respect to risk management, which of the below statements is true?

A. AWS does not formulate a strategic business plan; the client is solely responsible for risk control and risk management.

B. In order to define threats and enforce controls to reduce or handle those threats, AWS has established a strategic business plan. Customers do. not have to create and manage their own risk management programs.

C. In order to define threats, AWS has built a strategic business plan and has developed controls to reduce or handle those threats. Customers must also develop and maintain their own risk management plans to ensure that they comply with all relevant controls and certifications.

D. Neither AWS nor the customer need to worry about managing risk, so no plan is needed to be developed on both sides.

11. For the safe distribution of AWS Cloud services, the AWS control environment should be in place. In the collective control setting, which of the following is NOT expressly included?

A people

B. Energy

C. Technology

D. Process

12. In an AWS environment, who is responsible for setting up security groups?

A. The customer and AWS are ollectively responsible for ensuring the correct and stable configuration of security classes.

B. AWS is responsible for ensuring the correct and stable configuration of all security classes. There's no need for clients to think about setting up a protection squad.

C. Neither AWS nor Customer is responsible for configuring security groups; security groups are intelligently and automatically configured using traffic heuristics.

D. AWS provides Security Group as a Service functionality, but the Customer is responsible for the correct and secure configuration of its security groups.

13. Which of the option is NOT a recommended approach for customers seeking strong compliance and governance for a full IT control environment?

A. Take a holistic approach: Review the information available on AWS along with all other information and document all compliance requirements.

B. Verify that all control objectives have been met and that all significant controls have been designed and are operating effectively.

C. Implement generic audit objectives that are not specifically designed to meet their organization's compliance requirements.

D. Identify and document controls from all third parties.

Answers to Review Questions

1. A, B, C. Answers A through C define legitimate methods used by AWS to communicate with customers about its protection and control environment. AWS does not provide direct access to AWS data centres, facilities, or personnel for customer auditors..

2. C., The shared responsibility model, can include IT controls, and it is not limited to security considerations. Therefore, answer C is correct.

3. A. AWS provides IT control information to customers through either specific control definitions or general control standard compliance.

4. A, B, D. There is no such thing as a SOC 4 report, therefore, answer C is incorrect.

5. A. IT governance still remains the customer's responsibility.

6. D. Any number of workload components can be migrated to AWS, but it is the duty of the client to ensure that the whole workload remains consistent with different certifications and certifications from third parties.

7. B. There are several discrete data centers in an Availability Region, each with its own redundant power and network / connectivity, therefore, B is the right answer.

8. A, C. AWS periodically scans and notifies relevant parties of public-facing, non-customer endpoint IP addresses. AWS does not scan client instances, and clients need to ask for the right to conduct their own scans in advance, so responses A and C are accurate.

9. B. AWS publishes information publicly online and directly to NDA customers, but customers are not expected to share

information about their usage and configuration with AWS, therefore, B is right answer.

10. C. AWS has developed a strategic business plan, and clients can also build and sustain their own risk management plans, so C is the correct answer.

11. B. The collective control environment involves the individuals, processes and technologies required to build and sustain an environment that supports the AWS control framework's operating performance. Energy is not a part of the control environment that is discretely defined, so B is the correct response.

12. D. Customers should ensure that all the configurations of their security group are suitable for their own applications; response D is therefore correct.

13. C. Customers should ensure that they enforce control targets that are tailored to fulfilling the specific compliance criteria of their company, so C is right.

Chapter 6

Conclusion - Architecture Best Practices

AWS Well-Architected platform helps cloud architects create a secured, powerful, resilient, and efficient infrastructure for their applications and workloads. Operational excellence, protection, reliability, performance quality and cost optimization are the five pillars which AWS is based. AWS Well-Architected platform provides a cohesive approach for customers and partners to assess architectures and implement scalable designs over time.

The AWS Well-Architected Framework started as a single white paper but has expanded to include domain-specific goals, hands-on labs, and the AWS Well-Architected Tool. Available for free in the AWS Management Console, the AWS WA tool provides a mechanism to regularly review your workloads, identify high-risk issues, and record your improvements.

AWS has an ecosystem of hundreds of Well-Architected Partner Program members. You can engage a partner in your area to help analyze and review your applications.

Differences Between Traditional and Cloud Computing Environments

In a traditional IT environment, a company must deliver capacity based on the best peak traffic estimate (for example, Black Friday).

This implies that for a long time, a substantial part of the power can effectively be wasted.

This is the reason why Cloud Computing was created for your own use; you can use the extra strength garnered from others (in the case of AWS-Amazon). It is possible to start and stop servers, databases, storage, etc. in hours or even minutes, as needed.

Cloud computing with AWS has four main advantages:

It provide services when they are needed using the overall AWS infrastructure to physically deploy your applications closer to users (in a traditional model, you have to create your own data centers where the users are located); a host of managed services suggests that you can focus on building your product, and the low complexity is eliminated by being able to design AWS for a specific amount and you have the ability to track how much your organization spends on each service.

Design Principles

Scalability

An IT architecture can be scaled in two ways:

Vertical scaling – which involves upgrading from one source. This shows that it can take up more RAM, a faster processor or more storage capacity. This is a valid approach, but to a limit, an infinite number of RAM cannot be added to a disk.

Horizontal scaling- scaling from a number of sources. It sounds easy on paper (just get more servers), but not all applications and architectures are designed with a horizontal approach in mind, which makes it tricky.

Stateless applications

In stateless applications, horizontal scaling is ideally suitable. A stateless application is an application that does not require knowledge of the previous request sent to that application and does not store any information about the session as such. If you are more familiar with functional programming, a stateless application is essentially a pure function that delivers the same output with the same input.

There are two key approaches involved in sharing the workload between different devices, which are easier said than done:

- Push Model-To disperse inbound traffic to many instances where your application is running, using an Elastic Load Balancer (ELB). You can also use Amazon Route 53 (a DNS service) to implement DNS touring, but this is not an elastic solution and has its limitations.
- Pull model: Store action items in a queue (Amazon SQS) and instruct authorities to retrieve their own action item.

Stateless Components

Most apps are not 100% stateless; they store some sort of status information (for example, they need to know if the user is logged in so they can select the content specific to that user). You can still make some of these architectures stateless by not storing anything which persists in the local file system longer than one request.

You can use HTTP cookies to store session information, but not only do cookies have to be sent with every request, they can also be forged on the client-side.

Saving a specific session ID in an HTTP cookie and storing more comprehensive user data on the server would be a better approach. A stateful architecture is generated by storing the data on the server, therefore, the main solution is to store this data in a database (a DynamoDB is a good choice).

Shift the data to a storage tier framework like Amazon S3 or Amazon EFS if you have to deal with massive files, which will help you avoid stateful components.

Stateful Components

There are apps specifically designed to run on a single machine (for example, real-time multiplayer games that require extremely low latency). If you're developing such an application, you don't want to distribute traffic horizontally to any instance.

A recommended approach for HTTP/HTTPS traffic is to use the Application Load Balancer 's persistent session feature to bind a user's session to a specific instance.This ensures that, as long as they keep playing, they are not moved to another physical machine. In other cases, you may want to implement client-side load balancing. This introduces additional complexity, but may sometimes be necessary.

Disposable items instead of fixed servers

You can purchase physical servers in a conventional hardware environment, install them in a data center, and place them there manually to update packages., etc.

With AWS, you ultimately treat servers and all other components as temporary resources, providing them only when needed.

To deliver different identical (or very similar) sources swiftly, you can use:

- Bootstrapping - a script that you configure when provisioning, for example, an EC2 instance. It runs as soon as you initiate the instance, and it is possible to specify configuration details that vary between different environments (e.g., staging and production).
- Gold Pictures - Some AWS resources (EC2, RDS, and Elastic Block Storage EBS) can be created from a gold picture, which creates a snapshot of a resource at a point in time. This approach is generally faster than booting an instance and allows you to quickly and reliably boot additional resources by essentially "cloning" an instance.

- It is possible to configure an instance and save its configuration to create an AMI (Amazon Machine Image) - you can then start as many instances as you like by using it. In AWS, multiple AMIs are open, so before you build your own AMIs, check if your case has been resolved.
- Containers are also an option - Docker (with Amazon ECS - Elastic Container Service) is supported, so also Kubernetes (with Amazon EKS).
- There is also a hybrid model in which some parts of the configuration are captured in a gold image, while others are dynamically configured via startup scripts. AWS Elastic Beanstalk follows this pattern - it allows you use AMIs to initiate a new service and perform bootstrap actions via .ebextensions files, as well as environmental variables.

Infrastructure as Code

Infrastructure can (and should) be stored as code and version control. AWS CloudFormation templates allow you to create, manage and update resources in an orderly and predictable manner. This simplifies the reuse of architectures, as well as the extension of existing architectures, which is very useful for large organizations.

Automate

Traditionally, someone has to manually respond to incidents to increase storage capacity, deploy additional servers, etc. With AWS, it is possible to automate these steps.

Examples:

Auto Recovery for Amazon EC2: You can build a CloudWatch alarm that tracks and recovers an EC2 instance automatically in case anything goes wrong. It is far better than manually restarting the machine.

Autoscale: You can scale the number of EC2 instances, DynamoDB capacity, ECS and EKS as needed based on the desired capacity. This way, you're not running more shifts than necessary (wasting money) or fewer shifts than necessary (which will not keep up with traffic if there's a rush). It is better to schedule the autoscaling group launch for a while, so you don't have to wait for AWS to "notice" more traffic.

Use alarms and events: For example, create a CloudWatch alarm that sends an SNS message when a certain metric exceeds a certain threshold. These messages then take up a lambda function, sends a message to the SQS queue, or sends a request to the HTTP or HTTPS endpoint so that you can respond to the event in context.

Printed in Great Britain
by Amazon

54876506R00102